Children and Christian Initiation:
Leader Guide

Kathy Coffey

Living the Good News
a division of The Morehouse Group
Denver, CO
in cooperation with
The North American Forum
on the Catechumenate

Living the Good News
    a division of the Morehouse Group
Editorial Offices: 600 Grant Street, Suite 400
Denver, CO 80203
1-800-824-1813

Printed in the United States of America

Illustrations: Anne Kosel
Photographs: Mark Kiryluk, cover; Skjold Photographs, pages 17, 49, 64, 87; Marilyn Nolt, pages 9, 56; Catholic News Service (Michael Hoyt, page 80; Karen Callaway, page 72; Jacque Brund, page 40; The Crosiers, page 28)

Cover Design: Val Price

ISBN 0-889108-87-1

Contents

The Process of Christian Initiation (diagram) 6

Introduction 7

1 The Spirituality of Children 9
Contemporary Experience 9
Ancient Heritage..10
Hidden Mysteries of Childhood 10
Developmental Stages...12
Learning Styles...14
Experiential Approach...15

2 The Vision of Christian Initiation 17
Common Questions 17
Building Blocks of Initiation 21
Overview of the Four Periods 26

3 Launching the Initiation Process 28
Director's Role 28
Involving Parents..29
Recruiting the Team 31
Tapping the Community's Resources...32
Peer Companions 34
Sponsoring Families 34
Sponsors...35
Creating the Environment 35
Sample First Session...36
Structuring the Community's Involvement (chart)...39

4 The Rites of Christian Initiation...40
Rite of Acceptance into the Order of Catechumens 41
Rite of Election 44
Penitential Rites (Scrutinies) 45
Easter Vigil...47

5 **Minor Rites and Ritual Gestures** 49

Children and Ritual 49

Blessing 50

Anointing 51

Laying on of Hands 52

Presentation of the Creed 53

Presentation of the Lord's Prayer 54

Lenten Ritual 55

6 **Period of Precatechumenate or Inquiry** 56

Purpose of the Period 57

Echoes of Emmaus: A Precatechumenate Paradigm 58

Sample Session with Children: Family Issues 59

Sample Family Session: Power Over/Power With 61

7 **Period of Catechumenate** 64

Purpose of the Period 64

Rites of the Catechumenate 65

Celebrations of the Word 65

Service 65

Sample Celebration of the Word of God: The Call to Discipleship 66

Prayer 69

Sample Family Session: Epiphany 70

8 **Period of Purification and Enlightenment** 72

Purpose of the Period 72

Traditional Practices 73

Key Symbols—Water, Light, Life 74

Sample Purification and Enlightenment Session: Passion (Palm) Sunday 77

Ephphetha Rite 78

Preparation for Triduum 79

9 **Period of Mystagogy** 80

    Purpose of the Period 81

    Reflection after the Easter Vigil 81

    Sample Mystagogy Session: Promises...81

    Sample Session on the Sacraments 84

10 **Beyond Initiation**... 87

    Jessica's Continuing Journey 87

    Community Bonds 88

    The Uses of Enchantment...89

    Catholic Means Universal 89

    Empowering the Parents..90

    Continuing Apprenticeship 90

Resources for Further Reading 91

Glossary 92

Calendar of Celebrations 94

Period of
Mystagogy

Celebration of
of Sacraments
of Initiation

Period of
Purification
and
Enlightenment

Rite of
Election

Period of
Catechumenate

Rite of
Acceptance

Period of
Precatechumenate
or Inquiry

The
Process of
Christian
Initiation

Introduction

Are you thinking about beginning or continuing a process for the full sacramental initiation of uncatechized or unbaptized children in your parish? Then this is the book for you. You may hesitate because you've heard that the catechumenal process can be messy, confusing and a lot of work. All three complaints are probably true.

But you also may have heard that it can be a blessing in your parish. You know that the adult catechumenate world-wide has been a source of renewal for the church. The catechumenate with children has the same potential. Yet relatively few parishes have tried to implement it. This book should give you the knowledge and confidence you need to try. The rest is grace. Welcome to a wonderful adventure.

While old assumptions about faith development no longer hold true, and some strategies have become outmoded, other things stay the same.

Children's love of God, quest for meaning, desire for affirmation and need to belong don't change. If anything, the stresses on children have driven them to look more intently to God for a source of hope. So in God's name, we embrace, befriend, bless, anoint and invite them to service. We appeal to their imaginations with rites and to their senses with a conviction that the most ordinary thing can be a sacrament of God's presence. We arouse their wonder at a God revealed through waterfall and wave, taco and tamale, hug and hum, people and parakeets.

Rather than lament social upheaval, we adapt. Children used to hands-on education in school squirm if given lectures and worksheets by catechists. So we welcome children with a variety of experiential activities that lead them joyfully into our scripture and tradition.

A new era calls for a new paradigm. *The Rite of Christian Initiation of Adults* (hereafter referred to as *RCIA* or the *Rite*) offers that rarity of a new approach with ancient roots. After the Second Vatican Council restored the catechumenate for adults, we saw its benefits not only to those being initiated, but also to the whole community. Now we are starting to see it implemented with children. The *Rite* is a rich treasure; anyone leading the process of Christian initiation should read it and know it thoroughly.

Part I, #36-251, outlines the vision and general principles of the rite "in its complete and usual form"; Part II, #252-330, describes the initiation of children. For anything not found in Part II, look to Part I.

This resource is a practical companion designed to "flesh out" the guidelines of the *Rite*. It is intended for a director or coordinator of Christian initiation or team member, and provides:
- background on children's spirituality
- an overview of the vision of children's initiation
- tips on getting started
- an introduction to the rites and ritual gestures of Christian initiation
- practical applications: a summary of each period in the process and sample sessions for children and families
- a glossary of terms. For any bold word in the text followed by a star (*), turn to the glossary on page 92 for a definition.

This book is for the initiation director, coordinator or team member. Companion resources are the parent and sponsor guide, and initiation journals for children (age 7-10) and youth (11-14). Order these from Living the Good News at 1-800-824-1813.

The material is drawn from the experience of successful directors who have implemented this process, as well as the research of those who have formulated the underlying philosophy. It includes activities that catechists have found successful and that children have enjoyed doing. Thus, it translates the vision into reality. (Following the usage of the *Rite*, this book will refer to "children" while aware that teenagers will also be participating in the process.)

Those who still hesitate might consider that some old approaches to catechesis no longer serve us well. As we look into the faces of children who come in hope and trust, we must respond with the attitude of the young mother who explained to her daughter why she worked so hard for justice. "I will look at you, directly at you, and say I tried."

The Spirituality of Children

"As she followed her father down the passage Arietty's heart began to beat faster. Now the moment had come at last she found it almost too much to bear. She felt light and trembly, and hollow with excitement." —*Mary Norton, *The Borrowers[1]

At the age of ten, Jessica stands poised on a threshold, feeling the same excitement as the fictional character Arietty. Jessica is entering the process of Christian initiation, a unique blend of contemporary experience and ancient heritage.

Contemporary Experience

It helps to know Jessica's background. She had been best friends with Lupe ever since first grade three years ago. They lived in the same neighborhood, went to the same school and took turns spending Saturday night at each other's house. Both families were accustomed to the sight of Jessica's auburn braid beside Lupe's glossy black hair, bending over a project together.

Sometimes, Jessica went to church with Lupe on Sunday, and there she realized that Lupe's family had something her own family lacked. While her mom and dad were good people, they did not belong to any formal religious tradition. They saw Sunday morning as a welcome relief from the hectic, dash-to-work schedule of other days.

Jessica is entering the process of Christian initiation, a unique blend of contemporary experience and ancient heritage.

Jessica probably does not know that she steps onto an ancient path, renewed and enriched within the last twenty years.

At Lupe's house, Sunday morning meant church, and Jessica enjoyed being squished in the car with the whole Montoya family. At Mass, she liked to hum along with the music, smell the incense, hear the stories and watch the sunlight on the flowers. When the community prayed for homeless, hungry or warring people all over the globe, Jessica sensed a much larger world than her own small orbit of school, mall, playground and home.

While Jessica felt that Mass was meaningful and enjoyed participating, she also felt a little sad. She wanted to be part of this group, but at the same time, she knew she didn't belong to it. She envied the way the Montoyas' religion with its stories, beliefs, attitudes, celebrations and practices gave meaning, order and variety to their family life. Jessica asked questions that her mom couldn't answer from vague memories of Sunday school. Finally, after a particularly moving midnight Mass on Christmas Eve, Jessica told her mom she wanted to have what the Montoyas had.

Jessica's mother talked it over with her husband and after much discussion, approached Lupe's mom. The two women talked, then Jessica's parents met with the parish coordinator of initiation. Thus, Jessica was invited to begin, with her family, the process that would lead to full initiation in the Catholic Christian community.

Ancient Heritage

Jessica probably does not know that she steps onto an ancient path, renewed and enriched within the last twenty years. She begins the process as did Euphemius, a hypothetical ten-year-old of the late fourth century. Aidan Kavanagh describes Euphemius's initiation at the Easter Vigil.[2]

Purposely not told what to expect, the boy is almost drowned in the baptismal pool, gasps for air, is anointed with an enormously expensive oil whose fragrance fills the room, leads the procession to eat bread and drink wine and milk mixed with honey. Damp, oily and fragrant, Euphemius carries a terra-cotta lamp to symbolize that he represents Christ newly risen in his new life. Kavanagh concludes: "Euphemius had come a long way. He had passed from death into a life he lives still."[3] Sixteen centuries later, Jessica will have a similar initiation.

Hidden Mysteries of Childhood

Meeting Jessica for the first time, an initiation director might see scraped knees, disheveled hair and freckled face. Yet familiarity with a child's spirituality, development and learning style provides insight into a rich inner world. It is toward that hidden mystery that the whole **initiation*** process is directed.

Jesus appreciated the mystery of children's spirituality. He welcomed children. He blessed them and taught that unless adults receive the kingdom of God as humbly and responsively as a child, they cannot be part of the kingdom (Mark 10:14-16).

Eternal Questions

The realm of children's spirituality is vast. Yet those who prepare children for initiation would do well to begin by adapting the stance of Robert Coles, the author of *The Spiritual Life of Children*. Coles advocates humility before children's exquisitely private moments of "awe and wonder and alarm and apprehension." His research was rewarded when he abandoned one-sided inquiry and joined in speculative conversation. Similarly, the appropriate model of the initiating church is a big ear, reverently inclined toward the child.

Coles' research found that children ask the eternal questions: Where do we come from? What are we? Where are we going? Although they may give no external indications, children have thought long and hard about who God is. Various forms of "Kids' Letters to God" are perennial favorites because, beyond their humor, the children hint at deep truth.

"Children are messengers from a world we once deeply knew, but we have long since forgotten."[4] At times children take refuge in silence, wisely understanding that they cannot express the inexpressible. A deep sigh of satisfaction after hearing a scripture story can be their prayer, "Thanks be to God." Their silence can speak through gesture, art, recounting a dream. Quiet or seeming apathy can camouflage a lively inner landscape. Initiation directors are often astonished by the children who appear to have been bouncing around the room, not paying attention, but then reveal profound insights.

Longing for God

Researchers who work and write in the area of children's spirituality explore principles that shed light on the process of Christian initiation. For example, children's spirituality is not necessarily proportionate to their environment. In other words, the child of atheists may seem drawn to God more than the child of practicing Catholics. Children know things about God that no one has told them. Sofia Cavalletti found many children, growing up without religious influence or education, can express profound convictions about God. Abundant evidence led her to believe that the young child has a special attraction to and union with God.[5]

It is natural for children to long for love, and to find an infinite source in the God who is love. Since children are drawn so directly to God, adults can learn from them and abandon structures that are often superfluous.[6]

While any relationship with God is mystery, children try to tether the mysterious to the concrete, finding heaven and hell right here in daily life. Coles cites the example of an eight-year-old girl whose religious convictions helped her endure hateful racial warfare. She reported that as segregationists screamed at her, "suddenly I saw God smiling and I smiled."[7]

When a child uses innovative language about God, it is a sign that he or she is probably thinking independently. For in-

It is natural for children to long for love, and to find an infinite source in the God who is love.

The symbols and rites of initiation speak to the mystery of a child's spirituality.

stance, Theresa described Jesus' mission: "It was no picnic, his visit here."[8]

Relation to Church

Children's sense of morality is based more on everyday actions than on church attendance. Twelve-year-old Martin, interviewed by Coles, said, "People will fight—then with their friends, they hold hands. It's what you *mostly* do that counts, I guess...Even if a [person] doesn't go to church, he can be religious, because he's doing what's right to do."[9]

David Heller suggests that children are less interested in attendance at formal liturgies than in the quality of belief expressed in everyday ways. A lengthy, boring Mass is often punctuated by the wail of a child: "How long will this last?" Or, as a puzzled Hallie said, "We light candles on Fridays, but I don't really understand why." Heller cautions against making children "the small marionettes of religious theatre, acting...a prepared script."[10]

Children resist the efforts of formal religious instruction to block original or unconventional views and discourage discovery.[11] Asked to fill in a worksheet about the Trinity during an evening catechetical session, nine-year-old Ryan protested. "But I did these for six hours in school today! I don't want to do another."

Research also tells us that children should be helped to focus less on the expectations of others, more on their expectations of themselves.[12] For instance, Coles at first thought the Hopi girl Natalie was rude. She paused for long stretches during their conversation to observe hawks overhead. Yet when she shared her insights (and de-

tails Coles had missed), he felt like the rude one, pushing her to discuss her spirituality instead of letting her experience it.

Relevance of Research to Initiation

Summarizing the research on children's spirituality can help the initiation director to incorporate the following points as he or she begins the process:
- Listen to the silence of children as well as to the questions and insights they express.
- Trust the children's openness to God.
- Relate all activities and discussions to the everyday experiences of life.
- Understand that the symbols and rites of initiation speak to the mystery of a child's spirituality.
- Believe that the relationships built during initiation are helping to form each child's life of faith.

Developmental Stages

Since the *Rite* is clear about a "conversion that is personal and somewhat developed, in proportion to their age" (*RCIA*, #253), it is important to understand the different developmental stages of those in the initiation group. Like any guidelines, they are general and should be adapted to fit the individual.

Ages Seven and Eight

Young children are fostering a relationship with Jesus as friend and brother. He is their savior; they respond in a heartfelt way to his redemptive coming as a child. As Robert Coles points out, Jesus is "often presented in church as a child, one who for a long while lived as other children do—in relative obscurity, with a family. Moreover, he was a child who later had an important mission, and for many children, intent even at eight or ten on finding out what the future holds, Christ's life stands as a concrete example."[13]

Furthermore, children this age are natural ritual-makers. Anything they do once becomes a tradition: "We've always done it this way!" Thus, through participation in ritual they come to understand more than they can articulate. (See chapter 5, "Minor Rites and Ritual Gestures.")

Seven- and eight-year-olds display a great curiosity about formal conceptions of God. Their questions about God are triggered by particular issues in their own lives. They also express the desire to feel special, often because of the birth of younger siblings who claim a large share of parental attention. They are beginning to develop a sense of loneliness within the family as they realize that the family cannot shield them from every unknown and cannot meet every need. Their concepts of God are directly related to their interpersonal relationships, especially to the parents' absence or attention.

Ages Nine to Twelve

Nine- to twelve-year-olds are often concrete thinkers who can reason about their lived experience and can generalize about cause and effect relationships. Their growing relationship with Jesus enables them to make connections between Jesus and their daily lives. Furthermore, as Coles explains: "When children flounder a bit psychologically and morally, Jesus turns into a personal guide: he has been where I am, and so he knows, and he will lead me to an outcome in this life and in an afterlife, that is 'good,' that need not be feared."[14]

Children this age may see God as a stern judge or rule-maker. This image can be broadened by presenting stories of God as wind, mother hen, potter, bread or vine.

Ten- to twelve-year-olds may know more religious information, but also have stronger doubts. As they develop firmer self-images, they are increasingly aware of life's uncertainties. Perhaps because they feel less protected by their parents and see their families as less idyllic, they fear pain or suffering. They may ask elemental questions such as:
• What is God's role in suffering?
• Why does God allow pain?[15]

Much formal theology centers on these questions. We can affirm children's musings by telling them that many great thinkers have struggled with the same issues. We honor Job, Martha and Thomas in scripture for their role as holy doubters. Jesus accepts us with all our unresolved questions. Furthermore, he is a "God who weeps with us" and feels our pain.

As children become more aware of their limitations, they ask whether God has any limits. They hope that God can compensate for the things they cannot do. In the same vein, children who come from difficult family situations find that God meets deep needs their homes fail to satisfy. "This does not mean reducing the religious fact to a substitute for what life sometimes does not give; instead, it means that the religious reality responds to what our human nature indispensably needs."[16]

As children become more aware of their limitations, they ask whether God has any limits.

One little girl who had been sexually abused by her father, rather than turning from the image of God as father, loved the divine Father who would never hurt her.

Ages Thirteen to Seventeen

Thirteen- to seventeen-year-olds are dealing with many difficult issues, including puberty, identity questions, their own emotional roller-coaster and the growing recognition of suffering in the world. Unless spirituality is relevant to these issues, it will take second place. If scripture has no bearing on immediate problems, it is likely to be dismissed. Pat answers are suspect. Honest admission of doubt is preferable.

The very challenges of this age group can work *for* the catechist. Adolescents' enhanced cognitive abilities can contribute to their religious development. They are better able to grasp abstractions, to construct theories. Their idealism leads them to search out role models and reject hypocrisy. Often critical, argumentative and egocentric, they rise to the challenge to think for themselves. Starting to believe in their own uniqueness, they can come to a personal, owned faith. They may be starting to communicate with a personal God. Developing a keen sense of right and wrong, they willingly make short-term commitments to service projects.[17]

While achieving independence of family is a developmental task of adolescence, recent research shows that parents remain the most important influence in a teenager's life. The Search Institute of Minneapolis studied 273,000 young people to identify assets that would provide security and contribute to healthy development. The top three were all related to the love, support

> **The process of initiation offers young people the chance to challenge and test Christian faith as they seek to make it authentically their own.**

and advice of parents or primary caregivers.[18] Asked why he was joining the Catholic Church, fourteen-year-old Russell attributed his interest to the mornings he spent with his dad at "Sunday Lunch Bunch," making sandwiches for the homeless.

The process of initiation offers young people the chance to challenge and test Christian faith as they seek to make it authentically their own. Appropriate discussion questions with them are:
- So what difference does this make, anyway?
- Do you really believe this or not? Why?
- Where in your life outside of this group have you dealt with this issue this week?

Learning Styles

Jessica's learning style is her personal window on the world. It determines how she thinks, makes judgments and experiences people and events. Three typical learning styles:
- *auditory*—learning by hearing and speaking
- *visual*—learning by seeing
- *kinesthetic/tactile*—learning by moving and touching

The most effective catechists offer varied activities for all the different learning styles in a group. School systems often make the mistake of concentrating on one style (usually the visual or auditory). The kinesthetic learner may be given short shrift in sessions that demand long stretches of sitting and listening. (The sample sessions in chapters 6–9 offer activities that appeal to each learning style.)

Experiential Approach

Contrast the following scenes of two cate-chists breaking open the word with chil-dren in the process of initiation. Maya reads them the story of Jesus feeding thou-sands with a few loaves and fishes. As she discusses it, some children join in eagerly, while others glance at the clock, tip their chairs, or examine the shoe styles of the other children. Maya concludes by asking the children to memorize a verse from the story. Some are ready to recite it in a few minutes; others are starting to act out their boredom and irritation.

On the other hand, Bessie begins the same story by asking the children to help knead and bake bread dough in the kitchen of the parish center. She then asks them to name their favorite kinds of bread and to listen carefully for the role that bread plays in the story.

After telling the story, Bessie divides the group into two teams to run a relay race. At one end of the room is a basket of cut-out fish shapes. On each shape is a word from one verse in the gospel. A player from each team runs to the basket, pulls out a "fish"

and dashes back to his or her team. The first team to put all its words in order wins.

After the game, the children choose an ac-tivity. Some make a scroll, using shelf paper and markers to illustrate the story. Others divide into pairs. In each pair, one member plays the role of the boy who gave his lunch to Jesus and the other plays the boy's friend. The boy tells the friend what happened when he went to hear Jesus. Then they reverse roles. The first group then hangs their scroll, and one pair from the second group presents their roleplay.

Finally, a couple of children fetch the bread from the kitchen. By now it is warm and fragrant; they share it in the closing prayer ritual. Joining their parents, some children recount the race and others the roleplay, but *all* remember, engraved upon their senses, the story of Jesus who provides abundantly for all people.

Sometimes catechists find it difficult to be-lieve they are accomplishing anything through such an approach. Aren't the kids just playing? How will they learn anything?

"Play is a child's prayer."[19] Children's joy in everyday miracles, their spontaneity and total presence to the moment are qualities that adults work long and hard to culti-vate. If we question the primacy of play, we need only remember David dancing be-fore the ark or Miriam playing her tam-bourine, scriptural figures of child-like de-light in the Lord.

Through play, children are learning more than adults suspect, but more importantly, they are integrating it. To present children with already formulated doctrine invites only one, cognitive response: learn it.

I hear and I forget.
I see and I remember.
I do and I understand.
—*Chinese proverb*

The Catholic tradition is rich in signs that point to greater realities: water and bread, wine and light, leaven and oil.

Those who memorized the *Baltimore Catechism* can attest to the lack of personal involvement in this approach. If we suggest that belief is settled and codified, we leave nothing for the individual to do. Rather, we invite children to enter the mystery, bringing their gifts of imagination, creativity and sensitivity. They then can form a relationship with God that is more than intellectual, a unity with God that is bone-deep.

Children who respond to this approach are modeling adults. Andrew Greeley's research on Catholics who remain in the church shows it's the sense appeal (the smells and bells), not the doctrine that keeps us coming back. The Catholic tradition is rich in signs that point to greater realities: water and bread, wine and light, leaven and oil. As Sofia Cavalletti says, "the sign is a poverty that holds great richness and contains in itself the 'scandal of the Incarnation.'"[20]

The theory is made concrete through two examples:
- Mixing yeast into dough, Bianca entered into the parable of the leaven as she explained, "I am watching how the kingdom of God grows."[21]
- Brooke finished her whole worksheet on the Trinity while the little boy on her right struggled to complete the first blank. Despite Brooke's skill, she clearly considered it a meaningless exercise, politely asking the catechist, "Where's the trash can? I want to pitch this."

On the other hand, there was no question of trashing the pretzel she had made to symbolize the arms folded in prayer. Brooke had carefully rolled and shaped the dough, then happily devoured her pretzel when it emerged from the oven.

There is a marvelous affinity between children's spirituality and the rites and ritual gestures of the initiation process. To children longing for a God with skin, the church responds with the beauty of word, gesture and song, the wonder of mystery, and the assurance of God's constant, loving presence.

Notes

1. Mary Norton, *The Borrowers* (NY: Harcourt Brace, 1952), 58.

2. Aidan Kavanagh, "A Rite of Passage," ed. Gabe Huck, *The Three Days* (Chicago: Liturgy Training Publications, 1981), 107-110.

3. Kavanagh, 110.

4. Alice Miller, quoted in Jean Fitzpatrick, *Something More* (New York: Viking, 1991), 46.

5. Sofia Cavalletti, *The Religious Potential of the Child* (Chicago: Liturgy Training Publications, 1992), 31-32.

6. Cavalletti, 44.

7. Robert Coles, *The Spiritual Life of Children* (Boston: Houghton Mifflin, 1990), 19.

8. Coles, 208.

9. Coles, 171.

10. David Heller, *The Children's God* (Chicago: University of Chicago Press, 1986), 135.

11. Heller, 136.

12. Heller, 135.

13. Coles, 209.

14. Coles, 209.

15. Heller, 52.

16. Cavalletti, 172.

17. Gary Sapp, "Adolescent Thinking and Understanding," ed. Donald Ratcliff and James Davies, *Handbook of Youth Ministry* (Birmingham, AL: Religious Education Press, 1991), 70-96.

18. Peter Benson and others, *What Kids Need to Succeed* (Minneapolis, MN: Free Spirit Publishing, 1995), 24-31.

19. Jean Fitzpatrick, *Something More* (New York: Viking, 1991), 142.

20. Cavalletti, 160.

21. Cavalletti, 43.

Chapter 2

The Vision of Christian Initiation

Jessica and her family, along with the Montoyas, were invited to enjoy a picnic featuring barbecued hamburgers. There they met other children and families who were beginning the process of **initiation***. Leaving the park, they all felt encouraged, as if they had made a good start.

What they probably didn't know was that careful behind-the-scenes work of the initiation director and team had set the stage. This group had developed a process based firmly on the underlying foundation of the *Rite*. Others beginning the process need to understand its key components as they develop their own sense of vision for initiation.

Common Questions
What does initiation mean?

Any initiation is the process of bonding with a group. Those who are initiated take on a new identity. They learn the values, history, symbols, stories and celebrations of that group. In doing so, they develop a sense of belonging. The process is not foreign to children. They have joined a particular family, the Boy/Girl Scouts, the soccer or baseball team, a school community or a club.

Perhaps the best metaphor for initiation is what happens when two people become engaged. Gradually, they learn the customs,

Any initiation is the process of bonding with a group. Those who are initiated take on a new identity.

foods, humor, traditions and favorites of their future spouse's family. No one tests them on the complex network of relationships or the nuances of family expressions, but over a period of time, they absorb these and bring them to the creation of their own nuclear family.

Relationships are more important than learning a body of knowledge. The essential characteristic of God's people is not what they *do,* but who they *are.*

Who is eligible for this process?

This form of initiation is intended for children not baptized as infants, who have "attained the use of reason and are of catechetical age" (*RCIA,* #252). This usually translates to an age span of about seven to seventeen. However, some five- and six-year-olds are capable of personal faith and should be welcome. On the other end, some older teenagers might join the adult group.

Some children may have been baptized in another Christian tradition. It is important to honor the dignity of the baptized and to distinguish **catechumens*** from **candidates***. "The rite of baptism is held in highest honor by all Christians. Once it has been validly celebrated, even if by Christians with whom we are not in full communion, it may never lawfully be repeated" (*RCIA,* #4). Others may have been baptized in a Catholic Church but have not been catechized.

What makes Christian initiation unique?

This process invites children to experience God through Jesus within the Christian tradition and the church community. The hope is that knowing him, they will fall in love with him and begin a process that will continue throughout their lives. The essential dynamic is conversion. Because of their response to the gospel of Jesus, the children will participate in God's continuing activity through membership in the church, Christ's body on earth.

It is essential for this process that Jessica form relationships with people who will embody for her the Christian way of life. These relationships are more important than learning any body of knowledge. The essential characteristic of God's people is not what they *do,* but what they *are.*

What is the connection between the initiation of children and the initiation of adults?

The *Rite* for adults is the model, with appropriate adaptation for children. In practical terms, this means that children will celebrate the same rites as landmarks in their faith journey, but they will prepare for them and reflect on them afterward in different ways. (See *RCIA,* #252–330. For areas not addressed in Part II, Section 1 of the *Rite* [initiation of children] see Part I [initiation of adults].)

How does this process differ from traditional sacramental preparation?

Sacramental preparation has long followed an academic model with children in classroom settings grouped by age. The process of initiation is intergenerational and leads not to graduation, but to transformation. Through words, symbols and rites, the child is immersed in deep mystery. The liturgical assembly and the family context are the primary settings for initiation. The text is the scripture in the lectionary. While children learn sufficient information to make an intelligent commitment, their learning continues long after the initial reception of the sacraments.

Reconciliation Retreat ?
Eucharist Retreat ?

Thus, the process is holistic, not simply cognitive. "The *Order*...reminds us that initiatory **catechesis*** has more to do with seductive, loving relationships than dry notebooks and graded quizzes."[1]

The process reaches a peak in the reception of the sacraments of baptism, confirmation and eucharist at the Easter Vigil, then continues into the period of **mystagogy***. As Jessica leaves those "spine-tingling rites" fragrant with oil and nourished at the table, she does not have a sense of closure, but of beginning a life-long, ongoing commitment. Just as one never really exits a family of origin, so the hope is that through continued prayer, youth ministry, adult education and service, Jessica can stay linked to the Catholic family with which she has bonded so closely during her initiation.

How does a director work with the age differences?

If it helps, think of initiation in terms of a big, chaotic Catholic family. Despite different chronological ages and developmental stages, all absorb values, traditions and customs from the adults and each other. Sister Gael Gensler describes a group she directed in Wichita, Kansas, composed of fourth, seventh and ninth grade boys. They became a tight-knit trio, calling each other for one-on-one chats. In a Colorado parish, older adolescents took responsibility for younger ones in their group, introducing them at youth group and social events.

How does this group of children relate to other children preparing in the more traditional way for the sacraments?

The *Rite* calls for peer companions, baptized children of about the same age also preparing for confirmation and eucharist.

This becomes their "supportive setting of...companions" (*RCIA*, #254). All the parish's children can be brought together for special projects, such as making "ditty bags" for the homeless or preparing banners and wreaths for Advent celebrations.

What is the timing of the process?

Jessica's parents may ask: "How much time will this take?" They may be annoyed if the director of initiation seems to hedge. The response, "a year or two, maybe more" seems vague to people used to the definite durations of soccer season or school year. Because conversion is gradual and unique to each individual, it is difficult to predict a schedule. Hence, the length of the process depends on the needs of the child (*RCIA*, #253).

Ideally, groups meet weekly for at least a year, some for two years. The timing will depend on the needs of the child; some who are better catechized than others will need less time.

"Journey to the Fullness of Life," the U.S. Bishops' report on the implementation of the *Rite* in the United States, said that for parishes responding to their survey about children:

   8%— have a full-year initiation model
   27%—have a nine-month model
   13%—have a one-on-one model

The other parishes responding use either a different model, or have no children's process.

The year-round model is ideal because it avoids the awkwardness of trying to fit someone's conversion into the school year. Many directors have been embarrassed when approached by an earnest inquirer

The length of the process depends on the needs of the child.

For children, conversion means belonging, making their own the values and images of the Christian community.

who wants to start the process in May. It's hard to say, "wait 'til September!"

However, the reality is that the year-round model is hard to staff and run. Team members want the summer off; all participants take vacations. Some parishes have established a small pre-catechumenate team available during the summer for informal sessions. Since these team members will not be asked to serve during the academic year too, they are more willing to contribute their time in summer.

Another creative adaptation was developed by Diana Dudoit Raiche, a team member for the North American Forum on the Catechumenate. Parents in her group got so much out of breaking open the word with their children that they volunteered to keep their meetings going during the summer. An experienced catechist, Diana provided them with scripture background, reflection questions and activities for the summer Sundays. The parents who led the sessions reported learning as much as the children.

How can I address parents' concerns?

- Arrange for them to talk with someone who has already been through the initiation process.
- If possible, arrange for a sponsoring family to companion them through the whole process.
- Assure them that the family and child will be enriched by the process in which the child will receive all three sacraments of initiation.
- Provide parents and sponsors with the *Parent and Sponsor Guide* in this series, available from Living the Good News,

1-800-824-1813. This should answer many of their questions as they go through the process of initiation.
- Encourage them to reflect on whether it's really the right step for them to take.

Ultimately, only time and experience will calm anxieties that are hard to address at first.

Why are children being confirmed at different ages?

In the United States, confirmation has become a "rite of passage" usually celebrated during junior high or high school. *The Rite of Christian Initiation* calls for full initiation: baptism, confirmation and eucharist celebrated at once. So the child being confirmed may be younger than we usually expect. This may lead to confusion, but can be explained by a brief look at church history.

The *Rite* calls for a return to a much earlier practice that was common in the Roman church until the thirteenth century. What we know now as separate sacraments were once one: a single, unified rite of initiation, signifying full entrance into the Christian community.

To restore the ancient order, the *Rite* (RCIA, #305) mandates that unbaptized children receive baptism-confirmation-eucharist all at once. (The *Rite* forbids baptism apart from confirmation [RCIA, #215] because of the scriptural link between Jesus' baptism and the outpouring of the Spirit on his ministry.) Many parishes have adapted this change to children baptized in infancy, celebrating their confirmation and first communion simultaneously.

Some dioceses or parishes do not fully initiate children, but after baptizing them and giving them first eucharist, they delay confirmation to a later age. This practice violates the *Rite*, its U.S. statutes and Canon Law.[2]

While this approach is still being worked out, inconsistencies will plague the parishes. Children of different ages in the same family and children of the same age in the same class may receive the sacraments at different times. Admittedly, we are in a time of transition. But the *Rite* has been mandated as the *norm* for the church. All recent church documents call for the restoration of the ancient order, baptism-confirmation-eucharist. Practice follows slowly, hence we are temporarily caught in the inconsistencies that mark a time of transition.

Building Blocks of Initiation
Personal Conversion*

Any response to God's call must be made freely and knowingly. For children, **conversion*** means belonging, making their own the values and images of the Christian community. Furthermore, conversion should be developed in proportion to the child's age (*RCIA*, #253). It is geared to individual timing, not a program with one schedule to which all conform.

The most important focus of the initiation process is on learning the ways of Jesus. People who absorb his characteristics become more peaceful, compassionate and free. Children can learn contemplative practices in which Jesus' influence works upon the believer. The *General Directory for Catechesis (GDC)* defines authentic catechesis as more than mere instruction. It is an apprenticeship to Christ (#67).

No matter how messy the logistics become, our focus should be this: we put on Christ. All our efforts should be directed to one end: that the children we guide will someday say, "it is no longer I who live, but it is Christ who lives in me" (Gal. 2:20).

Through reading or hearing the gospel stories and relating to people who try to be Christ-like, they begin a journey which will last a lifetime. The security of belonging to the Christian community gives them the confidence to "go and do likewise," incorporating the patterns of Christ's life into their own. Paul describes this process: "and we all, with unveiled faces, beholding the glory of the Lord, are being changed into his likeness from one degree of glory to another," (2 Cor. 3:18). Through the Spirit, Jesus' human life in Palestine over two thousand years ago takes on new vitality and immortality in children who love and follow him today.

Family

The *Rite* (*RCIA*, #254.2) is clear that children seek initiation at the direction of their parents or guardians, or on their own with parental permission. Some parishes have found that the success of the initiation process is directly related to the involvement and support of the parents or guardians.[3]

Some children feel the first stirrings of faith in spite of parental apathy or alienation. The parents are the child's primary religious educators. But if parents choose not to be involved in the process, then the community assumes the role of nurturing mother.

> **I am all at once what Christ is, since he was what I am, and This Jack, joke, poor potsherd, patch, matchwood, immortal diamond, Is immortal diamond.**
>
> — *Gerard Manley Hopkins, "That Nature is a Heraclitean Fire"*

Initiation is the work of all the baptized, and functions best when everyone gets into the act.

Recent research on family systems has fleshed out the directives of the *Rite*. The *GDC* calls the family "the essential and first place where catechesis occurs. Within that circle, a child learns a positive view of being human, trust, freedom, self-giving and a joyful participation in life" (#178). The good news that came not in a book but in the person of Jesus continues to come through the human parent: his or her touch, laughter, lap, voice, fragrance and large embrace.

Andrew Greeley's research on the religious imagination has shown that people who image God as friend/lover/spouse rather than judge/master/lord see life as grace-filled gift. Their attitude is hopeful and positive rather than fearful and negative. Parents are the first communicators of these images, far more important than ideas because they are rooted at a psychic level deeper than knowledge or speech.

The research of David Heller confirms that children paint God as intimately involved in family life. He writes: "This deity is prominently and actively involved in family decisions and family tensions; [God] frequently helps to bring family members closer and helps them to stay together."[4] When children have anxiety about family tensions, they turn to God to restore harmony.

Community

The Rite of Christian Initiation builds on the ways a healthy community regularly brings its children into the fold. If the community is intact, it initiates its children naturally. After Mass, some parishes sing "Happy Birthday" to the birthday kids of the week; others applaud the t-ball victory or the scholarship. Those with financial resources buy the Boy Scouts' geraniums or the third grade's chocolate bars to finance the field trip.

Three examples show how easily and simply this can be done. During the prayers of the faithful at an African-American liturgy, a mother gives thanks for the life of a relative who died recently.

Her voice falters and she is overcome with emotion. Instantly, the arm of a friend reaches around her. With the slightest flicker of an eyebrow from dad, the woman's two children embrace her too. Encouraged by their support, she continues her prayer. Without a word, adults teach children how to comfort the grieving, how to be "the shelter of each other."

At a Hispanic parish, "los niños" have their own presentation of the gifts—con mucho gusto! Toddlers proudly carrying their dollar, older siblings bringing younger ones, tiny ones squirming in their parents' arms: all put their offerings in the basket at the front of the church while ushers circulate collection baskets to the adults. It is difficult to see how children could forget this ritual inscribed on their earliest memories.

After every Baptism at St. Francis Parish, the priest and parents process with the baby, wrapped in a white towel, from the font into the assembly. As the adults say the Creed, the children come to meet "the newest member of the family." They pat the infant gently, whisper words of welcome, and generally act like older brothers and sisters. Again, at the deepest levels the message is imprinted: this is how we act in this faith community.

The natural instincts shown in these examples are supported by research. The Search Institute of Minneapolis conducted a study of 273,000 young people to identify what assets would provide security and contribute to healthy development. The top three were related to the parents' role. But the fourth-ranked asset was the interest taken in children by other adults besides their parents.

How does this translate to a faith community?

Initiation is the work of all the baptized (*RCIA*, #9), and functions best when everyone gets into the act. The faithful community mediates the child's encounter with Christ and models an authentic Christian lifestyle. They create a saving network, bound by shared stories, symbols and celebrations to which the child wants to return again and again.

This role is especially important in a society undergoing radical change, where family systems are constantly failing and dissolving. Now that we realize how systemic sin affects children, we must build the antidote. To protect infants bombarded with evil from day one, "we need a community to bombard infants with grace from day one."[5] Just as in the early church, when Christians contended daily with threats that could be violent or fatal, so people today need each other's support if they are to live a faith that is countercultural. "In a pluralistic world of competitive values, families cannot go it alone."[6]

Liturgical Catechesis*

The combination of **liturgy*** and **catechesis*** is "greater than the sum of their parts." Together, the two can bring about conversion and transformation.[7]

For example, if Jessica hears the story of Jesus' welcoming the disciples to breakfast after the resurrection, sees people in the assembly welcoming each other, exchanges with them a sign of peace, prays for those who are hurting, eats at the eucharistic table, and sings "We Belong to the Family of God," she has received through several senses a powerful message about belonging. More formal teaching before and after the liturgy expands and deepens that experience.

There is long historical precedent for this approach, dating back to the gospels. In Luke's account of the Emmaus journey, the disciples recognized Jesus in the breaking of the bread. While they had heard about the resurrection, they came to understand it fully only in the context of ritual celebration.

The faithful community mediates the child's encounter with Christ and models an authentic Christian lifestyle.

Children's relationship to Christ springs from and is deepened by hearing God's word proclaimed and discovering its meaning for their lives.

The fathers of the church write of a process in which people enter the ritual with expectancy, have a rich, meaningful experience, then "unpack" its significance afterward. During the middle ages, the liturgy of the hours in the monastic communities kept the faith alive. The illiterate learned their faith from symbols decorating their churches. Stained glass windows made Christ tangible and the stories of his life understandable.

Today's media moguls know that to sell a product they must appeal to the imagination. How much of children's television is thinly disguised advertising, playing on the child's vivid fantasy? Paul Philibert proposes that the process of initiation can "landscape" the child's inner terrain with deep, archaic symbols. To the child's needs for affirmation, meaning, touch and inclusion, the church responds with "the symbols of God's presence and love."[8] Our children are surrounded by Walkmans and televisions, VCRs and MTV, yet the church's treasures can speak as loudly: calling the children forth for service, cherishing their gifts, and signing them with the cross. Verbalism cannot compete with the media; only the church's ritual wisdom can counter the media on their own ground, the field of the imagination.

Lectionary Catechesis*

The **lectionary*** is the church's way of dividing liturgical time. Through the annual cycle of lectionary readings from God's word, "the church unfolds the entire mystery of Christ," from his birth through his public ministry, his crucifixion through his resurrection, ascension and gift at Pentecost.[9]

The children's relationship to Christ springs from hearing this word proclaimed. Children in the initiation process move from their own initial response to a particular gospel story, to a group-sharing that broadens their personal interpretation, to a consideration of "What does this gospel call us to do?" and lastly to an experience of prayer.

The question often arises whether lectionary-based catechesis is "enough," if this approach will convey adequate understanding of doctrine and tradition. The answer is complex:

- Catholic doctrine and sacraments spring from scripture, not vice versa. Thus it is natural that the nativity readings lead to a discussion of incarnation, that Jesus' baptism would elicit a discussion of the baptismal commitment, that his call to forgiveness introduces the sacrament of reconciliation, that during Lent the paschal mystery is explored.

- Jesus taught by doing—healing, forgiving, eating with the marginalized, intervening on behalf of the outcasts. When he spoke, he told stories. Rather than present a paper on the dysfunctional family, he told the parable of the prodigal son. Rather than expound the doctrine of divine providence, he painted the images of lilies in the field. Instead of analyzing the problem of human suffering, he suffered on Calvary. Lectionary catechesis simply follows his lead. Jim Dunning writes, "If we teach as Jesus did, we tell stories—full of images and simple poetry interspersed with a few doctrinal one-liners that summarize the meaning of the stories."[10]

- During the rite of election, the question, "How much doctrine do they know?" is not the focus. Instead, the presider asks about the child's participation in the life of the community, prayer, service and dedication to the word.

- The view of sacraments as initiatory rather than end points opens a whole lifetime in which to reflect on their meaning and to learn church doctrine. The proper time for this kind of learning is *after* sacramental reception, not before.

Prayer

Since conversion is the primary purpose of children's initiation, the initiation process tries to facilitate the child's personal relationship with God. As in any relationship, a key component is communication. In the spiritual realm, we call this form of communicating *prayer*. "The *Order of Christian Initiation* emphasizes the importance of discerning the conversion of persons through their growth in prayer." [11]

A child's version of the traditional prayer types of prayer might be expressed as:
- WOW! (praise)
- OOPS! (contrition)
- THANKS! (gratitude)
- GIMME... (petition)

Surely God, like an eager parent, welcomes all the voices of God's children, no matter how hesitant they may sound. At this time, learning formulas for prayer is less important than encouraging the attitude of turning internally to God. Because prayer is so personal, it is helpful to offer a variety of prayer experiences from which the child can develop his or her own unique prayer.

Jessica learned to make the sign of the cross, join hands with others in her group to say the Our Father, listen to Jesus in silence, and praise spontaneously. Her catechist often had the children lead prayer, asking them, "What shall we thank God for?" Through retreats with her family, the ritual gestures that opened and closed each session, scriptural reflection and reinforcement from her parents and godparents, she gradually became a person of prayer. She learned to bring the challenges and the joys of her day to God in silence or in a few words. With her family's support and participation, she memorized a few lines from the psalms and the gospels that she found especially meaningful.

She learned how to relax physically and be still. Beginning with short periods of silence, she gradually worked up to longer times of quiet, nurturing her in a noisy world. All great religious traditions emphasize the importance of breath, a constant reminder of how God sustains us in life. So Jessica and her companions also learned to breathe deeply, let go of tensions, and let God enter in.

Service or Mission

From the beginning, the initiation process stresses striking a balance between contemplation and action. Prayer and scripture study flow into action; otherwise, the church runs the risk of becoming a privatized, therapeutic or "feel good" group; "something less than a Rotary Club with hymns."[12]

Jesus who fed the multitudes, cured the hopelessly ill and challenged the religious and political systems of his day says that his followers will do even greater things. The church that takes him seriously will

During the initiation process, children meet with a wide variety of prayer types.

explore the scriptures that cast light on social issues: poverty, unemployment, health care, refugees, military spending, housing, child and spouse abuse, judicial systems, environmental pollution and media exposure to violence.

Initiation is divided into four periods, which can occur at any time and for any length during the process.

Furthermore, the community will not be satisfied with study alone, but will move into active involvement. "We can have all the social encyclicals and pastoral statements we want...but who reads them? A handful of folks. Put a student from a middle-class family...into a St. Vincent de Paul pantry for one working session, then bring those students back and have a reflection time with them. You will find that they have been more impacted by what they did rather than what is available on their religious center library shelf."[13]

Breaking open the word sessions always explore the action that flows from the scripture. Most parishes offer many service opportunities with which children can help.

Overview of the Four Periods

Christian initiation follows the liturgical year (Advent through Ordinary Time) rather than the calendar year or academic year. Initiation is divided into four periods, which can occur at any time and for any length during the process. Rites mark the bridges between these periods. Ordinarily, the third period of preparation (called purification and enlightenment) coincides with Lent. The sacraments of initiation are celebrated at the Easter Vigil (*RCIA*, #256).

Period 1: Precatechumenate* or Inquiry
(*RCIA*, #36–40)

During this time, the community **evangelizes***, which means proclaiming the living God in Christ Jesus. The response is the "faith and initial conversion that cause a person to feel called away from sin and drawn into the mystery of God's love" (*RCIA*, #36-37). Children are introduced to various forms of prayer. After the initial contact and interview, **inquirers*** can meet every other week and families meet monthly. This period leads to the rite of acceptance or welcome.

Period 2: Catechumenate*
(*RCIA*, #75–105)

The goal of this period is to deepen faith through breaking open the word using the lectionary, participating in the community life of prayer and service, celebrating rites, witnessing to justice and loving others, even at the cost of self-sacrifice (*RCIA*, #75).

At weekly sessions to break open the word, some parishes like to have adults and children meet together. Others divide them into separate groups. Depending on the number of children involved, some then group the children by age. The families also meet together once a month. Participation in a parish outreach or service ministry begins, if this has not been a component from the outset. This period flows into the rite of election.

Period 3: Purification and Enlightenment*
(*RCIA*, #138–149)

This period usually coincides with Lent and the spiritual preparation for Easter. Weekly sessions emphasize the traditional Lenten practices of prayer, fasting and almsgiving as well as the gospels of Year A. There may be extra sessions in preparation for the **scrutinies*** and **minor rites***. Approaching the Easter Vigil, a morning, full day or weekend retreat may occur. This period leads to baptism-confirmation-eucharist.

Period 4: Mystagogy*
(RCIA, #244–251)

The **neophytes***, or newly baptized, continue to meet for a year until the first anniversary of initiation. During this time they break open the word and explore the meaning of the sacraments they have received. They continue with prayer, service and joyous community celebrations.

See chapters 6 through 9 for a detailed discussion and sample sessions of each period.

Notes

1. Maureen Kelly and Robert Duggan, *The Christian Initiation of Children* (Mahwah, NJ: Paulist Press, 1991), 41.

2. "Journey to the Fullness of Life." (Washington: National Conference of Catholic Bishops/U.S. Catholic Conference, 2000), 22.

3. Catherine Dooley, "Catechumenate for Children: Sharing the Gift of Faith," in Victoria Tufano, *Readings in the Christian Initiation of Children* (Liturgy Training Publications, 1994), 72.

4. David Heller, *The Children's God* (Chicago: University of Chicago Press, 1986), 25.

5. James Dunning, "Let the Children Come to Me: Christian Initiation of Children" in Tufano, *Readings*, 14.

6. Dunning, 18.

7. Sylvia DeVillers, *Lectionary-Based Catechesis for Children: A Catechist's Guide* (Mahwah, NJ: Paulist Press, 1994), 24.

8. Paul Philibert, "Landscaping the Religious Imagination," ed. Eleanor Bernstein and John Brooks-Leonard, *Children in the Assembly of the Church* (Chicago: Liturgy Training Publications, 1992), 23.

9. Thomas Morris, "Lectionary-Based Catechesis: Is It Enough?" *Catechumenate: A Journal of Christian Initiation* (September, 1991), 23.

10. James Dunning, *Echoing God's Word* (Arlington, VA: North American Forum on the Catechumenate, 1993), 61.

11. Kelly and Duggan, 94.

12. Aidan Kavanaugh, quoted in James Wilde, *Commentaries on the RCIA* (Chicago: Liturgy Training Publications, 1988), 41.

13. Richard Mauthe, Letter to the Editor, *National Catholic Reporter* (January 20, 1995), 36.

Chapter 3

Launching the Initiation Process

Reflect on how to adapt the *Rite* to your particular community.

Director's Role

The director of children's initiation faces challenges unique to each parish. In general, the task is balancing two things:

- The *Rite of Christian Initiation of Adults*
- The adaptation to the culture of a particular community

Before you begin the practical, hands-on work, you and your colleagues may want to reflect on what you are starting. Begin with personal memories of your own childhood. Discuss, think about or journal on the answers to these questions:

- What are your first memories of belonging to a group?
- How did this group welcome or reach out to you?
- Were there stages of belonging? costs to belonging? symbols of belonging?
- Can you name three formative events in your faith life as a child?
- What rituals of your childhood have carried into your adult life?
- What do you most want to bring children engaged in a process of initiation?
- How would you like them to answer the above questions?

Suggested Stages for Directors

I. Read the whole *Rite of Christian Initiation of Adults*, especially Part II for children.

II. Develop liturgical and catechetical structures to implement it.

  A. Liturgical

    1. Develop robust eucharistic liturgies and rites, in conjunction with the ordained clergy and liturgist.

    2. Use an effective liturgy of the word with children.

  B. Catechetical

    1. Introduce the whole parish to lectionary-based catechesis.

    2. Train catechists to:

      a) put the readings in context

      b) study background scholarship on the readings

      c) create ways to break open the readings

      d) share effective strategies with each other

III. Recruit and train a variety of ministers.

IV. Establish a strong Order of Christian Initiation of Adults.

In some ways, the director is leading a three-ring circus. Clearly, no one could do such a complex job single-handedly. Thus, it is vital to involve the parents, recruit an enthusiastic team and tap the community's resources.

Involving Parents

Jessica's parents are crucial to the initiation process: according to the *Rite,* "it is to be hoped that the children will receive as much help and example as possible from the parents" (*RCIA,* #254). Parents should not feel embarrassed by what they may perceive as a delay in bringing their children for baptism. If parents feel confident and competent, they will continue to support their child's religious development.

The initial interview with the family is crucial. The best place to conduct it is in the home, where the family is comfortable on its own turf, and the director can gather insights on the family's situation. If the interview is not appropriate in the home, then hold it at the parish.

Questions like these can be used during the initial interview.

- Who is asking for initiation?
- What does initiation mean to those who ask for it?
- Is there anything unusual about your child or your family situation that we should know?
- Will work schedules or joint custody arrangements make it difficult for you or your child to attend sessions?
- In what areas could the parish staff help you? For instance:
  — child care for younger siblings
  — antagonism of other family members
  — introductions to others in the parish
  — help with transportation
  — a chance to talk about your own faith issues as parents?
- What are the ages of your children?
- Where do they live? (for example, with one or both parents, stepparents, grandparents, guardians?)
- How many siblings will approach initiation?
- What school(s) do the children attend?
- What has been their religious experience? with faith in the home? When did they last attend Mass?

It is vital to involve the parents, recruit an enthusiastic team and tap the community's resources.

Make parents feel welcome, in the spirit of the baptismal rite: "The Christian community welcomes you with great joy."

Other issues may emerge in the course of the conversation, without taking the form of direct questions. Gathering this information early will help in planning the first precatechumenate sessions:

• Why are you interested in having your child initiated now?

• Which adults in the family are most interested/least interested in the process?

• In the case of a divorce/remarriage, what is the relationship of the custodial parent to the other parent? To what extent will the other parent be involved?

• What life issues are most pressing for your family?

After the interview, you may wish to make notes for yourself, considering:

• Is there any circumstance to which I should pay special attention here?

• How will this information be helpful in the initiation process?

Sensitivity to children and parents means avoiding settings where they might be embarrassed by their lack of religious vocabulary or experience. With large numbers of participants, arrange several groups of unbaptized, uncatechized children by age. With smaller numbers, combine different age groups or join resources with a neighboring parish. Or try an intergenerational approach, where parents and children work on a service project, skit, upcoming liturgical celebration or carnival together.

Richelle Pearl-Koller points out that parents who have been inactive in church are often surprised to discover that it has changed in their absence. "So, before even beginning to work with their unbaptized catechetical-age child, we ask the parents to take all the time they need to become comfortable and at ease in returning to their own religious practice and worship."[1] This may take a year before the child is actually enrolled in the initiation process.

Depending on their particular situation, the parents may fit into the parish's Re-Membering Church group or its Order of Christian Initiation of Adults. Some may join the parish's sessions preparing parents for baptism or first eucharist. Each situation is unique, so some parents may work with a catechist or small group, others with an individual sponsor or a sponsoring family.

Parents' first hesitancy (sometimes anger) can change gradually, but often the rite of welcoming marks a turning point. The first public rite may still be embarrassing, but as they sign their child, they begin to understand that they have embarked on an important process. As Father Don Neumann says, "People who have borne a burden of guilt for years may find absolution when the rite praises them as exemplary models."[2]

How does a director invite parents to participate actively, rather than simply "drop off the kids"?

• Make parents feel welcome, in the spirit of the baptismal rite: "The Christian community welcomes you with great joy." Parents should be embraced with open arms, without any judgment of their timing or their hesitancy. Directors can assure them that they may have been busy with other valid concerns: supporting their children financially, establishing a stable home or relationship, honestly examining their own beliefs. Their circumstances may differ radically from those of families where children are baptized as infants.

- Introduce parents to others like themselves. Realizing that "I'm not the only one in this boat" is a principle that has worked for many support groups, and helps build parents' sense of security.
- Have special ministers of hospitality stay in contact with parents regularly, asking, "How's it going?" Have other hospitality ministers make snacks, coffee, etc., available for parents at sessions.
- Hold some sessions with all the parents together, to carefully consider their questions and interests.
- Hold other sessions with parents and children together, structuring activities that involve parents in doing things with their children. Together, parents and children can participate in parish activities that help them learn what Catholics are about: for instance, working at a soup supper or potluck to benefit the homeless, studying and becoming active in a local justice issue, taking sandwiches to a neighborhood shelter, visiting a retirement center with the eucharistic minister, helping the liturgy committee decorate the church, singing in the choir, etc.
- Respect the fact that a family system is complex; probably no one can fully understand another family. Family values, relationships and traditions differ and are impossible to judge. There is no single, "correct" way to be family.
- The parent(s) usually act as the child's sponsor(s) during the rites (*RCIA*, #260).
- Buy the *Children and Christian Initiation Parent and Sponsor Guide,* available from Living the Good News, 1-800-824-1813. It will give parents and sponsors activities to do at home and build their confidence about their role in the process.
- Buy each child a journal in which to record their initiation process: initiation journals, available from Living the Good News, 1-800-824-1813. Two age levels (for children, ages 7-10, and youth, ages 11-14) provide activities that help catechists and save time for parents and sponsors.

Recruiting the Team

When Jessica came home from her initiation meetings, she talked about Marin and Marty, Phuong and Hidai. Her mother, remembering her own schooling, expected to hear about the rosary and the sacraments. Instead, Jessica's chatter was full of the retired couple who brought brownies, and the college student who led the first game. Why?

Just as the African tradition models the whole village's role in raising a child, so the community plays a key role in the Christian initiation of children. With all its warts, it still serves as a welcoming, nurturing family. As much as possible, have catechists and sponsors who look like the children; that is, they come from the same ethnic and racial backgrounds as the kids.

The child's instinct to belong is a strong one, as we have seen by the proliferation of gangs and the attempts of television to woo children. "Buy these jeans and eat this cereal; then you'll be *in*," is their not-so-subtle message. The church can also send children a strong message about belonging. The initiation director models that no one works alone, but with the support of a team to offer individual attention and relationships.

The first representatives of the parish community that Jessica met were members of

Consider recruiting college students, recent graduates, parish grandparents, singles.

If your parish is ethnically diverse, be sure that all different backgrounds have representation on the initiation team and a voice in its leadership.

the initiation team. Team members can serve as catechists in breaking open the word sessions, and as ministers of hospitality. In recruiting them, try to expand beyond the tried-and-true volunteers, the parish regulars who are already responsible for other clubs and activities and are probably short on time. Think of inviting recent college graduates or local college students (contacted through the campus ministry office or Newman Center) to work with those of junior high or high school age. Consider the parish's grandparents whose grandchildren live in another city. The parish singles who often feel excluded from family-oriented activities are another fine resource. If your parish is ethnically diverse, be sure that all different backgrounds have representation on the initiation team and a voice in its leadership.

You may also choose to have a precatechumenate team that serves only for the initial phase, at whatever time of the year an inquiry group is ready to start. They can specialize in the initial interviewing, and be sure that at least one of them who has met the family at home is present for the family's first visit to a session at the parish. This does not demand a large time commitment, thus, people may be more willing to commit on a short-term basis.

In the initial meeting with the team, discuss:
• What are we trying to do in the first phase of this process? (Make people feel welcome.)
• Describe times that you went somewhere with your family or alone and felt welcome—or not welcome. What can we learn from those experiences about what to do and what not to do with the children and their families?

• Complete this sentence: "Wouldn't it be great if we...?" (Welcome creative brainstorming!)
• What particular gifts do we bring to this process? (Help people discern whether they have time and talents for organization, art, catechesis, hospitality, music, baking, communications, leading a prayer service, befriending a child, or other ministries.)

Once the team has discerned its talents and placed its members where they can be most effective, the director is then free to float: visit sessions, train leaders, work with parents, serve as a substitute catechist. Not being anchored in any one part of the process, he or she can empower others to carry it on.

Ongoing team formation is essential. Some opportunities are provided by the North American Forum on the Catechumenate (especially the Children and Christian Initiation Institute or the Beginnings and Beyond Institute with a track on the implementation of the rite for children) and by local diocesan in-services. For Forum information see their website: www.naforum.org, e-mail info@naforum.org, or call 202-529-9493.

Tapping the Community's Resources

Remember how you chose your vocation or career? Many people are influenced by a teacher or a person already engaged in that line of work. So we major in science because of a dynamic biology teacher whose enthusiasm was contagious, or become a geologist because a favorite aunt shared her passion for the subject.

The initiation process focuses not on *what* we give Jessica and her family, but on *who* we give her. The greatest resources for initiation are the people in the parish. Children are initiated more effectively by following the community's example, living in relationship with people and doing things together, than by learning a body of religious dogma.

The following example from St. Rose of Lima parish in Gaithersburg, Maryland, clearly shows the community's role. One Sunday morning, adults and children in the initiation process gathered with their families and sponsors, parents whose children were baptized within the last year, and children preparing for eucharist and confirmation—ninety strong. They listened to the proclamation of Luke 4:14-21, Jesus' "inaugural address." In it he promises "release to the captives and recovery of sight to the blind," freedom to the oppressed and the year of the Lord's favor.

Through a homily and discussion, they broke open the word together, and shared a light lunch. Then they prepared for the homeless shelter that would be housed in their parish that week. People chose to work at different stations. Among their options:
- writing letters of welcome to the homeless
- making a guided meditation on what to put in a care package for a homeless person
- decorating bags and boxes for the care packages

Afterward, the director gathered the children and asked, "Help us remember what we did here..." Although the children didn't use catechetical jargon, they had seen the gospel translated into active service. Belonging to a community that actively demonstrates its care for the marginalized, they had contributed to its efforts. They had played their part and would continue to do so as they collected items for the homeless during the week. Their example can be adapted to different customs and settings around the country.

With respect to your own community, inventory the strengths and unique gifts of the people. Then schedule shrewdly. Ask:
- When can this community gather?
- When are people working?
- At what times would meetings create the least amount of stress?
- What are the unique celebrations of this parish community?
- What are the advantages/disadvantages of combining our resources with those of a neighboring parish?

Children are initiated more effectively by following the community's example, living in relationship with people and doing things together, than by learning a body of religious dogma.

A Calendar of Celebrations, page 94, may be copied for families to use at home.

The Catholic tradition is rich in its heritage of feast days and fasts, the rhythms of the church year. To children, they represent order as well as delightful diversion from routine. A Calendar of Celebrations, page 94, may be copied for families to use at home.

The *Rite* has a clear expectation that children being initiated attend a weekend Mass. At that time, they break open the word together. Some parishes continue a catechetical session after Mass. For some communities, meeting after Sunday Mass is difficult because parents work on Sunday. For others, Saturday evening or a week night is preferable. Again, adapt to the needs of your particular community.

Peer Companions

The *Rite* suggests that children to be initiated belong to a group of children the same age, who are already baptized and are preparing for confirmation and eucharist. This then becomes Jessica's supportive group of companions (*RCIA*, #254).

While the relationship of peer companion to child being initiated is not always one-to-one, a director can make use of the child's initial friendships. For example, Jessica wanted to join the church because of her friend Lupe. During the family's first interview, ask, "Is there someone you'd like to invite to come with you?"

The determining factor is always "What is best for the children?" Sometimes, a small group of children being initiated will be enriched by the presence of several peer companions (for instance, five candidates and catechumens with three peer companions).

Some small parishes have an entire religious education class or youth group act as companions. But with larger numbers, adding peer companions to the sessions would make the groups unmanageable and make it difficult to give individual attention.

To identify potential peer companions, ask the parish school teachers or religious education director to provide names of children who are approximately the same ages as those who will be initiated. Explain that these children will serve as supportive friends. They do not necessarily need to be the straight-A students, but the children who are welcoming, reliable and willing to make a commitment to the process. Work with them ahead of time to explain their role: they should connect the children being initiated to the larger parish. They can then brainstorm different ways to do this. (For example, worship together, attend parish functions such as potluck dinners together, introduce the children to their own friends and families, work on a concert or service projects together.)

For teenagers, peer support is more important than for younger children. Tap the parish youth group, school of religion, or local high school or college for potential companions.

Sponsoring Families

Explain to the parents of peer companions that the parish is offering a new option—sponsoring families. They may still choose the traditional sacramental preparation in religious education classes for their children, but explain that as sponsoring families and peer companions to unbaptized children, they will journey through the process together. The peer companions will then celebrate the remaining rites of initiation (confirmation and eucharist) along with those being baptized. Explain that the children's preparation will not be done in a classroom setting (although they will receive appropriate information about Catholic beliefs), but through prayer, ritual, community activity, reflection on scripture and church teaching, and service to others.

Begin by inviting the sponsoring families to social events with the families of children being initiated. In the precatechumenate period, have family clusters meet together. Continue these family meetings once a month during the catechumenate period, while the children meet together weekly to break open the word.

If this approach is presented as an option rather than a mandate, the response is likely to be more enthusiastic. After several families have tried it, the "parish grapevine" can publicize that the new option is indeed a healthy and effective approach.

If a whole family wishes to be initiated, find another Catholic family with children of about the same age and offer them the opportunity to be an "initiating household."

Sponsors

When a parent does not want involvement with the initiation process, it becomes the director's responsibility to appoint an adult sponsor who will attend sessions with the child, companion the child outside of the sessions and accompany the child through the major rites.

Some possibilities are:
- a grandparent
- an older sibling who has already completed the sacraments of initiation (sometimes a half brother or sister through remarriage)
- a single person from the parish
- the parent of a friend

As the community puts its best foot forward to welcome newcomers, it calls forth a variety of ministries. The question confronting the director of children's initiation may well be how to structure the community's involvement. If the cast of characters seems overwhelming, use the chart at the end of the chapter (p. 39) for preliminary brainstorming or as an organizational device. In the blanks provided, fill in the names.

Creating the Environment

If you have put in place the human resources of the community, give some thought to the environment in which you will meet. Try to create a place where children feel at home, seeing people and objects which are familiar, hearing the language that is as close as possible to their own. Try to avoid an academic setting, but if you must use a classroom, arrange the desks in a circle rather than rows. Or push the desks back and sit on the floor with comfortable throw rugs or pillows.

Use a consistent focal point for prayer, perhaps in the center of your gathering circle. Drape the table with a fabric children might see at home: a serape, a weaving or kinte cloth. Arrange there some beautiful, natural objects or plants, candles, some-

Begin by inviting the sponsoring families to social events with the families of children being initiated.

The environment in your meeting space should mirror the children's cultural backgrounds.

times a Bible or seasonally appropriate object. Art should mirror children's cultural backgrounds: Our Lady of Guadalupe, a black or Asian Madonna or Jesus figure.

Sample First Session

The first gathering of families is an informal one. Its purpose is social: to meet the other families of children in the process, the team and sponsoring families. Try bringing to this and all subsequent sessions the music, art, foods and customs of the different cultures represented in your parish.

Materials Checklist

- invitations
- comfortable meeting place such as a home, backyard or park
- food and beverages, eating utensils, etc.
- name tags and markers
- list of participants, their addresses and phone numbers
- schedule of future meetings, parish events and Mass
- basic informational packet about the parish, including phone numbers of parish staff and initiation team
- clean-up crew

Ice-Breakers

Begin with a favorite opening activity, enabling people to relax and start getting to know each other. Two possibilities:

- *Color name tags.* Before the gathering, cut out an assortment of circles, squares and triangles large enough to write a name on them. Use a variety of colors, but make only a few shapes of each color. Supply a hole-punch and yarn to hang the name tag around each person's neck.

Ask participants to select the color and shape they want, write their name on the tag, then explain to the group why they chose the one they did. (For example: "I chose a circle because I'm always running in circles." "I chose red because I'm hot and thirsty.")

If you need an easy way to divide the group for discussion later, have participants form groups according to the colors they chose.

- *Catholic Bingo.* It's easy to get a chuckle over Catholics' favorite game as you hand everyone a sheet with a grid of three boxes horizontally, three boxes vertically. Each box should include a description or picture of common objects such as a hole in a sock, a watch, a braid, $1 bill, etc. Everyone in the group then tries to fill a row of boxes with names of people in the group who have the item in the description. Younger children may need help. The first to fill a row of boxes with names wins.

Family Stories

Rita Burns Senseman of Noblesville, Indiana, emphasizes family stories at her first session. To encourage families, ask them in advance to bring photo albums or to make posters that show pictures of family members and their favorite activities, foods, work, vacation spots, holiday traditions, etc. Invite family members to use their pictures and posters to introduce themselves to the group. Focus on:

- What makes the Montoya family unique?
- What unique gifts do Lupe, Ramon, etc., bring to this family?

Or, if families do not have time to prepare in advance, provide them with newsprint and markers at the session itself. Ask them to "map" their journey over the years, marking times when God seemed to be especially present with them. When the map is complete, have the children explain it to the larger group.

Bridge from this discussion to the family of God's people:

Parents who wish to get started can begin with the first 3 chapters of *Children and Christian Initiation: Parent and Sponsor Guide.*

- *In scripture.* Tell the story of Abraham and Sarah (Genesis 12:1-10). Point out how God called them, how at times they were fearful or uncertain, and how they kept going on the strength of God's promise. Draw the parallel:
  — God also calls us on a journey.
  — God called you here today.
  — You responded.
- *In the parish community.* If possible, invite someone who has been through the initiation process to tell the story of how it affected their family.

Explain that entering the initiation process marks the beginning of participation in a larger family, the parish and the world-wide church.

Housekeeping Details

Try not to burden people attending the initial session with lengthy schedules and de-mands that may seem overwhelming. (We may never know how risky it has felt for them to take this first step.) Instead, clarify the date of the next meeting and promise to stay in touch by phone.

Other details such as long-range scheduling can be handled by giving out packets with the relevant calendars or information. Try to include in the packet the names and phone numbers (office and home, if team members agree) of several contact people at the parish.

Notes

1. Richelle Pearl-Koller, "Initiation: An Event That Remembers Itself," in Kathy Brown and Frank Sokol, *Issues in the Christian Initiation of Children* (Chicago: Liturgy Training Publications, 1989), 81.

2. Don Neumann, *The Catechumenate for Children* (Allen, TX: Tabor Publishing, 1991), Videocassette.

Structuring the Community's Involvement

Children to be Initiated	**Peer Companions**	**Sponsoring Families**

Families to be Initiated	**Initiating Households**

Other Parish Resources

Groups to tap occasionally	Check	Area of Service
Youth groups		
Children in parish school or religious education		
Men's/women's groups		
Social justice committee		
Retirees' club		
Choir		
Singles' group		
Young marrieds		
Other		

Chapter 4

The Rites of Christian Initiation

> The rites of initiation plant the seeds of wonder at an imaginative level far deeper than most children can articulate.

"If I had influence with the good fairy who is supposed to preside over the christening of all children, I should ask that her gift to each child in the world be a sense of wonder so indestructible that it would last throughout life, as an unfailing antidote against boredom and disenchantments of later years, the sterile preoccupation with things that are artificial, the alienation from the sources of our strength."

—*Rachel Carson*[1]

The rites of initiation plant the seeds of the wonder Carson describes, at an imaginative level far deeper than most children can articulate. For many children, the beauty of music, art, gesture and poetry found in ritual will speak more a profound and lasting language than the more academic study of doctrine. Andrew Greeley's studies have shown that Catholics remain Catholic more because of their attraction to the images or "smells and bells" than because of any abstract dogma. To concrete-minded children, the movement of procession, the touch of oil on the skin and the blaze of bonfire communicate more directly who God is and who we are than book or lecture. Furthermore, the rites act as fulcrums, bringing what Jessica has already experienced into public expression, and at the same time strengthening her commitment to the process. The rites also bridge from one period to the next.

Here are some guidelines to remember as you plan the rites in cooperation with the parish liturgist:

- The symbols are eloquent. Let them speak without too much fuss or explanation.
- Respect the assembly's gifts and limitations.
- Understand the *Rite*, how this particular rite fits into the larger context and what adaptations are appropriate.
- Don't complicate things for the sake of novelty.
- Especially for children, music, art, environment, gesture and silence can say more than words.
- Welcome cultural expressions specific to your community.

Rite of Acceptance into the Order of Catechumens

(*RCIA*, #262–276)
This first public ritual, the rite of acceptance into the order of catechumens, marks Jessica's transition from initial inquiry to active involvement in preparation for the sacraments of baptism, confirmation and eucharist. During the rite, Jessica's parents present her to the community. This signals her entrance into formal preparation and the parents' acceptance of the responsibility to be actively involved in her religious formation.

The rite is often celebrated with the adults also preparing for initiation. "From this time on the Church embraces the catechumens as its own with a mother's love and concern" (*RCIA*, #47). The assembly expresses this message by going out to welcome the catechumens and candidates.

The authors of the *Rite*, concerned about children's shyness, suggest celebration with a small group, "since the presence of a large group might make the children uncomfortable" (*RCIA*, #260). The director of initiation is best suited to make this decision by asking:

- Will the children be intimidated or distracted by a large assembly?
- Are their parents embarrassed by the idea of a public ritual?
- Would this group feel more warmly welcomed in an intimate setting or a Sunday assembly?

In making the decision, consider two examples. Georgia Glover of Littleton, Colorado, finds a supportive community for this rite and arranges for its celebration in one of the following ways:

- During an Advent vespers service, with people who have recently been fully initiated and understand the rite's significance.
- In a prayer service with children the same age from the religious education program, who will later write letters of welcome to the children being initiated at the Easter Vigil.
- In the context of a teenage retreat or youth group meeting with an assembly of peers from the youth group or religious education.

Sister Gael Gensler expresses this view: "The children belong to the whole parish and all their rites should be celebrated with the adults, in the full context of the Sunday assembly." If there are large numbers of children, she repeats the rite at different Masses. The general practice throughout the country is to integrate children with adults for the rites. [2]

This rite is explained for parents and sponsors in the *Parent and Sponsor Guide*, pp. 36-38.

For a child's overview of all the rites and the questions before and after the rite of acceptance, see initiation journals, pp. 8-11.

Throughout the rite of acceptance, the robust primal symbols of bowing, touching and signing speak loud and clear.

Preparation

The general preparation for this rite is the period of precatechumenate. The specific preparation should *not* explain what will happen. The goal for all the rites is that children enter into them *fresh*, their senses alert and their imaginations awake, so the symbols can speak to them. Jim Dunning quoted "noted theologian" Katherine Hepburn, "A kiss isn't much of a kiss if you have to *explain* it, dahling"

The following questions should help Jessica articulate what she is looking for and define her commitment to the next step of the process.

General Questions

These questions may be used as aids in preparing for the rite, for discussion in a small group, or with a sponsor, team member or parent.

Remember a time you moved to a different city, house or school. (For children who have not had these experiences, it may help to discuss starting a new grade in school.)
- Did you feel lonely or worried about the move?
- Who welcomed you or helped you move into the new setting?
- How did you feel about the move when it was completed?

Questions on the Symbols
Community
- Name one person who has helped you come closer to Jesus. What is it about this person that helps you know the Lord?
- What do you look forward to doing or sharing with this person as you continue the process of initiation?

Scripture
- What is your favorite Bible story?
- Which character in the story is your favorite?
- Why do you think reading the Bible is important?

The Cross
- What hurts have you experienced?
- Name a person or group you feel sorry for because they are sick, lonely, homeless or hungry.
- How would you like to help this person or group?

While one team member rehearses the parents or sponsors in their role during the ritual (signing the senses, presenting the Bible and cross), another can prepare the children by reflecting on the questions they will be asked in the opening dialogue. (RCIA #264)
- What do you want to become? (Some answers might be: a Christian, a friend of Jesus, a member of the Christian family, a follower of Christ.)
- Why do you want to become a Christian?
- What do you gain by believing in Christ?

Depending on your group, you may have children prepare their responses in writing or in art by working individually with sponsors, or at home with parents.

Celebration

The parents or other adult sponsors present their children to the community at this rite, which is often celebrated with the adults who are also preparing for initiation. Throughout the rite, the robust primal symbols of bowing, touching and signing speak loud and clear.

Key Components of the Rite of Acceptance
Entrance into the Church

Some parishes have effectively utilized the symbolic value of having those to be welcomed gather outside the doors of the church. The community, prepared in advance, then comes outside, encircles the candidates like a womb and escorts them into the church, singing robustly.

Opening Dialogue (RCIA, #264)

Children (individually or as a group, depending on the number) are asked to express their intention. The celebrant will do so through questions similar to those listed above, then conclude by saying, "...We welcome you joyfully into our Christian family, where you will come to know Christ better day by day...."

Affirmation by the Parents (Sponsors) and the Assembly (RCIA, #265)

This brief dialogue underlines the responsibility of the parents and the adults in the community to support the children as they prepare for full initiation.

Signing with the Cross (RCIA, #266-269)

The sign of the cross traced on the foreheads of the children by the celebrant and parents or sponsors marks them as Christians and reminds them of Christ's love. (For older children, the *Rite* suggests signing all the senses, as with the adults. The gestures should be large enough for the assembly to see clearly. They should also be reverent, the expression of deeply held belief.) Some parishes also present the children with an actual cross, although this is not part of the rite.

Presenting the Bible (RCIA, #273)

Giving the children a Bible or a book containing the gospels is an option that can occur during the liturgy of the word, after the readings and homily. The reason for doing so is that the gospel is the heart of the learning for the catechumenate, the next period the children will enter.

Some parishes may give this book during a catechetical session. If possible, invite parents and sponsors to write a personal message to the child in the front of the Bible. Remember ecumenical sensitivity in presenting the Bible: some children baptized in other traditions may already cherish it.

Reflection After the Rite

In a session following the rite, discuss:
- How did you feel about the rite?
  — about standing before the community?
  — about the questions you were asked:
    Why do you want to become a Christian?
    What do you gain by believing in Christ?
  — about being marked by the cross?
  — about receiving the Bible?
  — about receiving the cross?

Anticipate responses such as these, gathered by Rita Burns Senseman:
- From a dad: "I felt humbled when bending down to sign the feet of my child."
- From Sandra: "I felt like Jesus was covering me [during the signing]."
- From Mike: "I felt big. When my parents bent down to sign my feet, it's like they were saying they would be loyal to me. I just felt like I was the big person."

For children's activities on the Rite of Election, see initiation journals, pp. 21-23.

To help parents and sponsors understand the Rite of Election, see the *Parent and Sponsor Guide*, pp. 38-41.

The discernment "chat," like every other step in the initiation process, should be marked by reverence for the child's spirituality and respect for his or her privacy.

Rite of Election

(*RCIA*, #277–280)

The rite of election marks the end of the catechumenate and the beginning of purification and enlightenment. It is usually celebrated within Mass at the beginning of Lent and marks the start of the final preparations for the sacraments of initiation. On the basis of the adult testimony and the children's reaffirmation of their intention, the Church makes its "election," or choice of the children who will become fully initiated. The importance of this rite is the declaration that God's choice of these children is eternal.

Many parishes celebrate a rite of sending to the larger gathering, the rite of election. Through this rite, the local community acknowledges the children's readiness to receive the sacraments of initiation. Key components of the rite:

• Children are called forth by name.
• Parents, godparents and the assembly give their affirmation of the children.
• Unbaptized children enroll their names in the book of the elect.
• The celebrant declares the children to be the **elect***** of God, chosen to be initiated at Easter.

The rite of election is celebrated on the First Sunday of Lent at a place such as the cathedral. It is a rite of such a serious public nature that the bishop presides, declaring the candidates and catechumens *the elect*, those chosen by God to celebrate the sacraments of initiation.

When all the people preparing for initiation gather together, it gives them a sense they may not have had before, of being part of a much larger and more universal church.

For children, it may be their first experience with a bishop or a cathedral. As twelve-year-old Michael remembers vividly, "I got to sit right beside the bishop!"

Preparation

Children discuss with a parent, sponsor or small group:
• Where have you signed your name or seen your parents sign for you? (on checks, report cards, letters, memos, library cards, loans)
• What does signing one's name mean?

The *Rite* prescribes an appropriate process of discerning whether children are ready (*RCIA*, #256). In this process, use the questions that the celebrant will ask the parents, godparents and assembly during the rite:
• Have these children shown themselves to be sincere in their desire for baptism, confirmation and the eucharist?
• Have they listened well to the word of God?
• Have they tried to live as faithful followers?
• Have they taken part in this community's life of prayer and service?

If the questions sound a bit heavy-handed for children, try what Georgia Glover calls "chats with children." In an informal, one-on-one conversation, she is often surprised to discover how much they have been absorbing through the process.

For instance, Matt was a rough-and-tumble fourth grader who spent many of the sessions bouncing around and fiddling with his baseball cap. Yet when Glover asked Matt what he'd been learning, he assured her solemnly, "I know that the angel asked Mary to do whatever God wanted. She did.

And I'm ready to do whatever God wants me to do."

They may also come up with original questions and insights beyond what their parents or catechists said. Glover reports that one mother had an "attitude" all year; she just wanted her children to "get communion" as quickly as possible. She rarely attended a session. But during the "chat" with the director, her second grader asked poignantly, "If Jesus died for me, what about my Jewish friend?"

The discernment "chat," like every other step in the initiation process, should be marked by reverence for the child's spirituality and respect for his or her privacy. Sofia Cavalletti suggests that children's exigencies or deep needs are met by the aspect of God that most corresponds to them.[3] Thus, it may be appropriate to ask a form of the Ignatian question ("What is your deepest desire?") adapted to children ("What do you most need?"). The response may indicate what face of God the child most needs now. For instance, if the child desires health, present Jesus the healer; if the child desires peace at home, present Jesus who died to bring peace to all.

Celebration

Members of the community prepare in advance to speak on behalf of the children. Parents, sponsors or peer companions talk briefly about the evidence of conversion they have observed in the child's life: perhaps faithfulness to prayer or service, kindness, a longing for Christ.

Then as the children's names are called, they come forward to write their names in the Book of the Elect. Richelle Pearl-Koller writes that she is always touched by the time and effort it takes for young children to complete their signatures. "Inscribing their name is like searing their memory with the great effort needed to live the gospel of Jesus."[4] And each week when they return to church, they see the book open to their names!

To Father Don Neumann, the Book of the Elect represents the parish record of those who have responded to Jesus' call. A child seeing his or her name there can say with pride, "Here's my name! I belong!"[5]

After they celebrate the rite of election with the bishop, adults and children preparing for initiation, along with their families, may want to gather for a pizza party or potluck back at their home parish.

Penitential Rites (Scrutinies*)

Because using the term *penitential rite* for children is confusing, this book uses the more appropriate term **scrutiny,** as it appears in Part I of the *Rite.*

The adaptation of the *Rite* for children (*RCIA,* #291–303) calls for at least one scrutiny, though they may have all three, as celebrated with adults. Sometimes the scrutiny also includes the celebration of first reconciliation by baptized children and peer companions who are preparing for eucharist and confirmation. The scrutiny recognizes the presence of sin and its effects on ourselves, our world, our church and our children. At the same time, it reassures us that Christ is more powerful than the worst evil. Furthermore, it shows participants that no sin is beyond the merciful forgiveness of Christ. He who cured the blind and lame can heal us.

For children's activities on the scrutinies, see initiation journals, pp. 24-26.

To help parents and sponsors understand the scrutinies, see the *Parent and Sponsor Guide,* pp. 42-45.

For children's activities
on the Easter Vigil,
see initiation journals,
pp. 27-30.

To help parents and
sponsors understand
the Easter Vigil,
see the *Parent and
Sponsor Guide*, pp.
45-48.

Preparation for Ages Seven to Twelve

Before this rite, children in this age group may discuss with a parent, sponsor or small group the following questions:
- What do you most wish you could do for others?
- What keeps you from doing this?
- Or, complete the blank: "I really want to do this_____, but even when I try, I can't."
- What do you really want to happen? What do you hope never happens?
- So what should we pray for? What can we ask Jesus to free us from?

If possible, try to incorporate the children's answers to the last question in preparing the scrutiny rite.

Preparation for Ages Thirteen to Seventeen

By this time, young people in their teens probably have a keen awareness of the world's evil, and of the evil in their own lives. Discuss with them:
- How easy (or hard) is it to avoid sin or evil?
- What are some influences on teenagers that might lead them to sin or do evil?
- What is the purpose of searching or examining our **consciences***?

Clarify what a scrutiny is, its purpose and effect. Ask the young people to contribute to the litany used in the liturgical rite for the following weeks.

First Scrutiny
Third Sunday of Lent:
- How do you thirst for God: in your relationships, your work or school, your quiet time?

- Where do you see people in our society thirsting for God? (abused children, the homeless, the ill, victims of injustice)

Second Scrutiny
Fourth Sunday of Lent:
- Where in your life do you find "blind spots," or places you can't seem to see clearly?
- What situations in our world most seem to need the light of Christ?

Third Scrutiny
Fifth Sunday of Lent:
- When do you feel dead, disappointed, bound or restricted, like a failure?
- Where in our world and our church do people still need to be freed? brought to life?

Celebration

If celebrated apart from the Sunday eucharist, within the liturgy of the word, the scrutiny consists of prayer, scripture reading, homily, intercessions, exorcism and anointing with the oil of catechumens (*RCIA*, #291–303).

Whenever possible, have the children do the readings, prepare the intercessions (using the questions above) and read them.

Reflection After the Rite

Discuss with a partner, parent, sponsor or small group:
- What part of the scrutiny touched you most?
- What did you learn from it about sin? about grace? about Jesus?

Easter Vigil

(*RCIA*, #206–243, 304–329)

Because of the close connection between Jesus' death and resurrection, and the initiation of children who are joined sacramentally to him, the Easter Vigil is the primary time to celebrate baptism-confirmation-eucharist (*National Statutes*, #18-19; *RCIA*, #308). Baptized peer companions may also celebrate confirmation and eucharist with the elect.

Preparation for the Children

In one sense, all of Lent is the spiritual preparation for the Easter Vigil. The children should become familiar with its key symbols through the readings and the discussion and activities that accompany them. In so doing, they should "enter a world brimming with sacraments, icons and images of God."[6] (See chapter 8, "Period of Purification and Enlightenment.")

Their "inner landscapes" thus sensitized, the children should be attuned to the meaning of the symbols they encounter in the spine-tingling rites of the Easter Vigil. Any attempts at rehearsal or explanation in advance would be redundant and counterproductive. But one practical note: tell parents of younger children that naps are essential. Often the Vigil goes late at night—no snoozing through their own baptisms!

Preparation for Sponsors, Parents, Team

To prepare the sponsors and parents involved in the rites, the director will want to walk them through to allay anxiety and shyness. The director, presider and team may also want to view in advance the videocassette, *This Is the Night*, with liturgist Don Neumann.[7] Keep in mind that the *Rite* allows "the greatest freedom" (*RCIA*, #35) for adaptation to particular circumstances, and that even rites not perfectly celebrated can still carry meaning. Perhaps the best preparation for director, liturgist, presider and all is to gather in prayer before the Vigil and invoke the grace of the Spirit.

Preparation for the Assembly

Show or post in a prominent place pictures of each person who will be initiated at the Easter Vigil. Have children in the parish or school religious education classes, and youth and adults in parish organizations, who have seen the pictures, write or draw letters of welcome to all the adults and children who will be initiated. Candidates and catechumens surprised by this outpouring of welcome find it quite touching. In one parish, a child wrote, "Welcome to our parish! Be sure to get to Mass early, or you'll have to sit on the metal chairs in back." Another wrote, "I've seen you at the rites in church and I'm praying for you."

Guidelines for Celebration

(*RCIA*, #566–594)

- Overview of the celebration:
  — Service of Light: blessing the fire, lighting the Easter candle
  — Liturgy of the word
  — Baptism and renewal of baptismal promises
  — Confirmation, with anointing and laying on of hands
  — Liturgy of the Eucharist
- Our symbols are robust, not puny. This means that a large congregation, straining to see, needs a huge bonfire (not a "liturgical hibachi"), sweeping gestures, abundant candles, lavish outpourings of water and oil.

Show or post in a prominent place pictures of each person who will be initiated at the Easter Vigil.

- Whenever possible, build in movement: from the fire to the readings to the water and eucharistic tables. Reassure the assembly, especially antsy children, that they can get up and move around if the readings become long; better yet, include a break for everyone.

- Some people think the children "upstage" the adults, but it's hard to resist the sight of them returning after their baptisms, clothed in white, to dress the altar with flowers and a cloth they have made and written their names on. What a powerful symbol of new life!

Reflection After the Rite

(See chapter 9, "Period of Mystagogy," and the material in the *Parent and Sponsor Guide* and initiation journals.)

Notes

1. Rachel Carson, *The Sense of Wonder* (New York: Harper and Row, 1956), 42-43.

2. "Journey to the Fullness of Life," #7.

3. Sofia Cavalletti, *The Religious Potential of the Child* (Chicago: Liturgy Training Publications, 1992), 172-173.

4. Richelle Pearl-Koller, "An Event That Remembers Itself," ed. Kathy Brown and Frank Sokol, *Issues in the Christian Initiation of Children* (Chicago: Liturgy Training Publications, 1989), 85.

5. Don Neumann, *The Catechumenate for Children* (Allen, TX: Tabor Publishing, 1991), Videocassette.

6. James Dunning, *Echoing God's Word* (Arlington, VA: North American Forum, 1993), 358.

7. Don Neumann, *This Is the Night* (Chicago: Liturgy Training Publications), videocassette.

Chapter 5

Minor Rites and Ritual Gestures

"All that we know, we know in deeper, richer, hidden ways beneath the threshold of language and words." —*Paul Philibert*[1]

When Jessica was nine, she read about the holocaust. She became frightened that the same thing could happen in this country, that some night her family might be torn from their home and shipped to a concentration camp. Although her parents tried to assuage her fears, they accomplished little on the level of talk. Her father wisely tried a ritual instead.

Once a month, he and Jessica walked to a particular tree in a park near their home. They admired the tree, ivory in moonlight and gilded by the late afternoon sun. They watched the cycle of buds to leaves to autumn foliage to bare branches. Month after month, the tree remained there. Touching it regularly seemed to soothe Jessica. Her father assured her, "The tree will still be here," but what he implied was far more important: "*You* will still be here." The whole vital message was communicated almost without words.

Children and Ritual

Children experience more through ritual than they can articulate. Their deep hunger for affirmation and meaning is met through the ritual signs developed in the

Children's deep hunger for affirmation and meaning is met through the ritual signs developed in the community of faith over the centuries.

For children's activities on rituals, see initiation journals, p. 18.

To help parents and sponsors understand rituals, see the *Parent and Sponsor Guide*, pp. 57-60.

community of faith over the centuries. "The child's nostalgia for being lovingly touched by the cosmic mother lives on in us. The church meets that nostalgia with washing, anointing, embracing, laying on hands, and gestures of reverence...These gestures have a symbolic resonance that can touch the depths of our yearning."[2]

When our young people want to be included, to be recognized as unique in a competitive world, we answer their hope by choosing, calling, welcoming, recognizing talents, missioning for service, inviting to join in action, and signing with the cross.[3]

Richelle Pearl-Koller transposes the natural instinct of children to make ritual into the process of initiation. What we are about in initiation is images, symbols and pictures of our faith: water, book, cross, oil, table, bread, people, candle, fire.[4] She uses the example of her adopted Korean daughter, initiated at age seven. She was baptized by the pouring of water from a huge, bright green bowl. A year later, seeing the same bowl at the Easter Vigil, the little girl shouted, "Hey, Mom, that's my baptism bowl!" Her mother reflected that her daughter's memory of baptism held that green bowl in her imagination.

The rituals in this chapter can be introduced during the catechumenate and continued throughout the process as a part of sessions to break open the word, family retreat days, etc. Also encourage the parents to introduce or continue family rituals informally at home.

For example, have one of the participants reverently light a candle at the beginning of the gathering. Play background music softly if it seems appropriate. Invite the whole group to sing or say "God is light; in God

there is no darkness at all" (1 John 1:5). At the end of the session, have another participant reverently extinguish the candle and say, "Go in peace to love and serve the Lord." After doing this several times, it should become one of the group's natural rituals.

One group began their prayer simply, by passing around a basket filled with shells or shiny pebbles and having each person take one. As each child offered his or her spontaneous prayer, he or she placed the shell or pebble back in the basket.

To explain parts of the Mass, provide plates, chalices, unconsecrated bread and linen cloths so the children can handle these items reverently. They can also learn the gestures of blessing the bread and wine, saying a phrase from the eucharistic liturgy, such as "Through [Christ] we ask you to accept and bless these gifts we offer you in sacrifice."

As you introduce other ritual gestures such as making the sign of the cross with holy water, holding hands to pray, blessing, anointing, and laying on of hands, be sure to explain these to the parents so they will adopt them at home.

Blessing

(*RCIA*, #95–97)

Lupe wouldn't think of leaving for school in the morning without a blessing. Every night as she goes to bed, her mother traces the sign of the cross on her forehead and prays softly over her daughter. For Lupe, regular blessings are a source of peace, order and security. All children deserve such a gracious heritage.

The tradition of blessing is an ancient one. In the Hebrew scripture, we read that when Abram left his familiar world to launch a journey in faith, God blessed him, saying, "I will make of you a great nation, and I will bless you, and make your name great, so that you will be a blessing...and in you all the families of the earth shall be blessed" (Genesis 12:2-3).

Today, many families bless their food with a table grace and sometimes unconsciously, we bless people who sneeze. What we are saying, though we may not realize it, is: May you have all good things, all the rich life that God wants for you. According to the *Rite* (RCIA, #95), "the blessings of the catechumens are a sign of God's love and of the Church's tender care." They are given so that those who do not yet have the grace of the sacraments can still be strengthened for a difficult journey.

You may want to make this gesture as simple as tracing the sign of the cross on the child's forehead while praying, "May God bless you and keep you." You may want to use a sung version such as Carey Landry's "A Prayer of Blessing" on the *Bloom Where You're Planted* audiocassette.

Anointing

(*RCIA*, #98–103)

In the children's book *Missing May* by Cynthia Rylant a little girl remembers: "Before she died, I know my mother must have loved to comb my shiny hair and rub that Johnson's baby lotion up and down my arms and wrap me up and hold and hold me all night long. She must have known she wasn't going to live and she must have held me longer than any other mother might, so I'd have enough love in me to know what love was when I saw it or felt it again."[5]

Rubbing a baby's skin with lotion will be familiar to children who have baby sisters, brothers or cousins. Others will quickly recognize the gesture as a sign of tenderness; help the children connect what they have seen at home with the ritualization they will experience at church.

Jessica will be lavishly anointed at the Easter Vigil, just as perfumed oil was poured over Euphemius until its fragrance filled the room.[6] She should also be anointed by her catechists and parents before that night, and grow into an understanding of what the symbol means.

We anoint children because they are "a royal priesthood, a holy nation, God's own people" (1 Peter 2:9). In ancient times, the kings of Israel were anointed. Jesus was anointed priest, prophet and king. To children who often feel small and powerless, anointing is a dramatic reminder of their royal heritage. Christ in his love invites them to be a priestly and noble people.

Child psychologists have underscored the importance of children forming a healthy self-esteem. The rite of anointing with its overtones of royalty surely enhances the self-image. When Jessica was anointed with fragrant oil, she explained to her mom that the perfume was expensive, which just showed how important *she* was!

Before the Anointing

Discuss with the children:
• How do we use oils at home? (for baking, motors, squeaky doors, bathing)

To children who often feel small and powerless, anointing is a dramatic reminder of their royal heritage. Christ in his love invites them to be a priestly and noble people.

• How does the church use oils? (for anointing the sick, the catechumens, the ordained)

During the Anointing

The children are initially anointed by a priest or deacon with the oil of catechumens at a formal session. Successive anointings can be done by their parents, sponsors or catechists, with a mixture of olive oil and perfume.

Mark the sign of the cross on the forehead with oil and pray:
• May your mind serve God with wisdom.

Mark the sign of the cross over the heart and pray:
• May God gift you with a sense of what it means to be held in love. May the wounds of your heart be healed, so you can gladly give and gladly receive.

Mark the sign of the cross on the hands with oil and pray:
• May God open your hands to serve others.

Laying On of Hands

Jesus embraces the children, blesses them and lays his hands upon them (Mark 10:13-16). The laying on of hands is one of the primary symbols that recurs throughout the process of initiation.

Frightened by inappropriate touching and saddened by the scandals of pedophilia, we may hesitate to touch children. Yet they may hunger for that touch. One solution is to follow Boy Scout guidelines: always have two adults present to protect adults as well as children.

We can also invite children to touch or hug each other. Furthermore, we can talk with children about the ways they like to be touched: a hug from mom, friendly head-tousling from grandpa, arm wrestling with a brother or sister. Finally, we can remind them that Jesus touched people he healed, and that he especially liked to touch children (Mark 9:36-37).

After reading a scripture passage such as those above in which Jesus touches someone, use the laying on of hands in one of these ways:
• as a ritual gesture within a celebration of the word
• as part of an opening prayer, asking God to enable us to listen well
• as part of a closing prayer, to enhance communication with family, friends and schoolmates during the week ahead

The catechist, parent or sponsor might lay one hand gently over each of the child's ears while placing the thumbs on the child's mouth, and pray in words like these:

• "(*Name*), may your ears and mouth be opened to hear and speak the faith that is growing within you. We ask this in Jesus' name. *Amen.*"

Presentation of the Creed

(*RCIA*, #157–162)

This **presentation*** usually occurs after the first scrutiny during the period of purification and enlightenment, but may also be adapted to a time during the period of catechumenate (*RCIA*, #104).

In preparation for this rite, discuss:
• What promises have you made as part of belonging to other groups? (Scouts, clubs, school or class covenants)
• Why do you think the church has a set of promises or a creed?
• What does the word *creed* mean? (Explain the derivation of the word: *creed* comes from the Latin *credo* meaning "I believe." It is a simple, stark statement of "Here I stand.")

Before the Presentation

Children should have some familiarity with the Apostles' Creed, revered as an early, concise set of statements about the faith. At Sunday Mass the assembly recites the Nicene Creed, formulated in A.D. 325. In a sense, children give it back to the community through the profession of faith at the Easter Vigil.

During the Presentation

A powerful way to communicate these creeds is by having the team, sponsors and/or parents encircle the children and recite them to the children. Then, they may present the children with copies of the creed beautifully lettered on parchment scrolls (available from your local church goods store—or enlist the aid of parish artists and calligraphers).

After the Presentation

While these roots are important, eminent theologian Avery Dulles challenges us: "A new creed should be designed to challenge the assumptions of the prevailing culture."[7] The Christian message is alive, vital and changing. Most Catholics today hold essential beliefs about the eucharist, liturgical life and justice that are not mentioned in past credal formulas.

Thus, children with the help of sponsors, family members or initiation team should think through what religious beliefs they hold most dear. They may be given some examples of creeds people have written in their own words. Older children and teenagers may like this Masai creed from Africa, discovered by Jim Dunning and shared in the "Beginnings and Beyond" Institute of the North American Forum on the Catechumenate.

> We believe in the one High God...
> God promised in the book of his word, the Bible, that [God] would save the world and all nations and tribes.
> We believe that God made good [that] promise by sending [the] Son Jesus Christ:
> A man in the flesh,
> A Jew by tribe
> Born poor in a little village,
> Who left his home and was always on safari doing good...
> He was rejected by his people, tortured, and nailed hands and feet to a cross, and died.

For children's activities on the creed, see initiation journals, p. 19.

To help parents and sponsors understand the presentation of the creed, see the *Parent and Sponsor Guide*, p. 41.

For children's activities on the Lord's Prayer, see initiation journals, p. 20.

He was buried in the grave, but the hyenas did not touch Him, and on the third day He rose from the grave...
We are waiting for Him.
He is alive. He lives.

After giving such an example, a sponsor or parent can ask each child to finish the sentence:
• I believe...

A group of children ages nine to twelve can fill a chalkboard or sheet of newsprint with beliefs that finish the sentence:
• We believe...

Ages thirteen to seventeen may want to design Creed Books, placing a phrase on each page, perhaps written in calligraphy or an elegant computer font.

Or, you may want to design activities that prompt children to reflect on each of the phrases of the more traditional Apostles' Creed. For example: "I believe in God, the Father almighty, creator of heaven and earth."

Discuss God's creative actions and God's ongoing care that sustains all creation. Consider these art projects to prompt children's reflection:
• *For individuals:* Draw something you created or care for (for example, a carpentry or sewing project, a map or poem, a pet or plant).
• *For groups:* Give everyone markers or crayons and mark each person's space on a long sheet of paper. Invite them to make a mural of God's creation, with everyone drawing what they love best. Encourage the artists to include themselves. As the group works, they can discuss:
— What do we like about God's creation?
— What do we like best about ourselves? (If any are shy, remind them that "God doesn't make junk.")

Presentation of the Lord's Prayer

(*RCIA*, #178–182)

This presentation may occur after the third scrutiny, but timing is flexible (*RCIA*, #104). Children from other Christian traditions may already know this prayer; therefore, the rite should be handled with sensitivity to them.

Options for the presentation:
• Divide the prayer into the following petitions and ask group members to choose one phrase each and to explain what it means to them personally.

— Our Father who art in heaven,

— hallowed be thy name;

— thy kingdom come,

— thy will be done on earth as it is in heaven.

— Give us this day our daily bread

— and forgive us our trespasses as we forgive those who trespass against us;

— and lead us not into temptation,

— but deliver us from evil. *Amen.*

• Rewrite each phrase in the language we use today.

• Provide a variety of art materials and ask the children to make pictures illustrating each phrase. Display them.

• Invite the children to express the prayer through sign language or liturgical dance.

• Discuss:

— Why do you think Jesus used this prayer to teach us to pray?

— How could praying this prayer each day make a difference in our lives?

Lenten Ritual

In the final preparation for full initiation, children move more deeply into the paschal mystery. Provide ways for them to pray or ritualize their new understandings. Two suggestions:

• Joyce Rupp, O.S.M., describes a ritual in which children who had experienced the death of a loved one during the previous year received a lit candle in honor of the person who died. As each child received the light and placed it on the altar, he or she told whom the light honored: "My grandmother, my dad, my friend, my brother..." She writes: "Tears filled my eyes as more and more lights sparkled

and twinkled upon the altar. I felt the presence of the ancestors, 'the wise ones...' I felt the strength of their presence and the power of their goodness."[8] Through the ritual, the children see that death isn't the final word. Even those who have died continue to bless us with their light.

• Bring both aspects of the paschal mystery to prayer through a bean bag with different colors on each side. Tell the group that one member will throw it to another. If it lands on the blue (*substitute your color*) side, the person who catches it should thank God for something that deserves praise. If it lands on the other (*red*) side, the person receiving it should present a petition to God, some problem needing God's intervention to solve.

In the final preparation for full initiation, children move more deeply into the paschal mystery.

Notes

1. Paul Philibert, "Landscaping the Religious Imagination," ed. Eleanor Bernstein and John Brooks-Leonard, *Children in the Assembly of the Church* (Chicago: Liturgy Training Publications, 1992), 15.

2. Philibert, 23.

3. Philibert, 23.

4. Richelle Pearl-Koller, "Initiation: An Event That Remembers Itself," ed. Kathy Brown and Frank Sokol, *Issues in the Christian Initiation of Children: Catechesis and Liturgy* (Chicago: Liturgy Training Publications, 1989), 80.

5. Cynthia Rylant, *Missing May* (New York: Orchard Books, 1992), 4.

6. Aidan Kavanagh, "A Rite of Passage" in Gabe Huck, *The Three Days* (Chicago: Liturgy Training Publications, 1981), 108.

7. Avery Dulles, quoted in Harvey Egan, *Leaven: Canticle for a Changing Parish* (St. Cloud, MN: North Star Press, 1994), 100.

8. Joyce Rupp, *Little Pieces of Light* (New York: Paulist Press, 1994), 59.

Chapter 6

Period of Precatechumenate or Inquiry
(RCIA, #36–40)

For children's activities on the precatechumenate, see initiation journals, pp. 1-9.

To help parents and sponsors understand the precatechumenate, see the *Parent and Sponsor Guide*, pp. 20-21.

The first stirrings of Jessica's faith came in attending Mass with her friend Lupe. Even before the period of precatechumenate, evangelization may have already happened outside a formal church setting. As the initial awakening moves into the larger context of the parish community, we honor God's call and presence in Jessica's life.

At the same time we recognize that she is beginning a long journey to full initiation. The setting for this stage will involve parents and possibly other sponsoring families, the children of these families forming Jessica's peer group. They should all understand that their role is to welcome and to befriend. Precatechumenate sessions may be held either at the parish or in homes.

During this period, it is important to pay close attention to Jessica's lived experience, the impressions and values that her family has given her. Jessica meets Jesus through the scriptures and through informal prayer. She and her family gather regularly with other children who are inquiring and with sponsoring families. The period has no set duration, lasting as long as Jessica needs to hear the stories and to formulate her desire to join this Catholic family.

Purpose of the Period

The inquiry period has several purposes:
- to form friendships (through family clusters, peer companions, social activities, etc.)
- to evangelize, or discover how Christ is important in peoples' lives (through their stories)
- to introduce the church's varied forms of prayer and encourage a life of prayer (by suggesting and modeling a different prayer form at each session)

The information and insights gathered during the family's initial interview are helpful for planning the content of these first sessions. (See p. 29 for specifics on the initial interview.) Since images of God are more fundamental to faith than ideas of God, the director will listen carefully to the children's stories of what God is like for them. For instance, children educated in a Catholic school, but lacking follow-up at home, may know religious doctrine and vocabulary, yet still be afraid of God. To these children, the good news may mean replacing these fear-filled images with that of Jesus as a loving friend. During the precatechumenate, it is important to present images from both the Old Testament and New Testament to enrich and broaden children's images of God.

Those who work on the precatechumenate team need the skills of eliciting peoples' stories and encouraging them to raise significant issues. Although the underlying questions of this period may not be phrased so directly, they are:
- Who is Jesus for you?
- How does God act in your life?

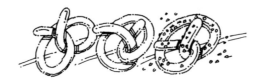

For an example, let's eavesdrop on Julie as she kneads dough with Jessica's group of nine- and ten-year-olds. She mentions that they are making pretzels, an ancient Christian symbol of prayer. Casually, as the children roll dough "snakes," she asks:
- "How do you pray?"
- Jessica answers, "At night, when it's dark and I'm scared, I ask God's help."
- "What frightens you?" Julie follows the child's lead.
- "Burglars." "Drugs." "Gangs."
- Jamal chimes in, "And spiders!" "My mean brother," Aaron adds. Softly, Rosa whispers, "I'm scared when my dad takes drugs."

From this conversation before she popped the pretzels in the oven, Julie gleans what issues disturb the children. Now her task is to bring these to prayer and link them to scripture. With the children, she will pray in various ways, trying to find which form is best suited to the different personality types of Jessica, Jamal and Rosa. (See *Please Understand Me* for the correlation between temperament and nourishing prayer styles.[1]) She tries to discern and honor each child's unique prayer life. Finally, she makes suggestions to the parents for family prayer at home.

TIP: Choosing a Meeting Place

Homes are usually a better setting for precatechumenate sessions, especially if your parish has small faith communities and other activities already meeting in homes. Sometimes a small group feels lost in a big church hall, or in rural areas people may have to travel long distances to the parish. However, the parish is an appropriate meeting place for people who feel uncomfortable about having a group in their homes or for groups too large to accommodate in a home.

In the past, some religious educators may have been guilty of giving the answers to children who had not even thought of the questions. Sometimes children may be more willing to share these with a peer companion.

Echoes of Emmaus: A Precatechumenate Paradigm

Father Frank Sokol finds in the journey to Emmaus (Luke 24:13-35) a paradigm for the precatechumenate.[2] He suggests we begin with Jesus' question to the disciples: "What are you discussing with each other while you walk along?" (verse 17). In other words, "What is your daily experience?"

What's Happening in Your Life?

Jessica's questions are the starting point. In the Indian tradition, the guru never begins by giving information that may be unwanted. The guru begins by asking, "What are your questions?" In the past, some religious educators may have been guilty of giving the answers to children who had not even thought of the questions. Sometimes children may be more willing to share these with a peer companion. Or, children who are not too articulate may express themselves more freely through art media such as drawing, painting or clay.

After each child has shared something of his or her story, have other children respond with a commonly known phrase that affirms the speakers and assures them they have been heard. For instance, "Be gentle when you break bread," or something scriptural in tone like, "Everything I have is yours already" or "When two or three gather in my name, I am there among you."

Areas to explore:
- Problems at home:
  — mom and dad fighting?
  — not enough money or time together?
  — sibling issues?
  — parents divorced, away from home, ill?
  — stressful schedules?
- Problems at school:
  — grades?
  — relationships with friends/class-mates?
  — sports and extracurricular activities?
  — prejudice?
  — teachers?
- Areas of joy or pleasure:
  — friends?
  — family?
  — hobbies, sports or activities?
  — pets?
  — nature?

Link to Scripture

When Jesus met the disciples along the road, they were depressed and confused. Their near-paralysis is evident in Luke 24:17: "They stood still, looking sad." After he listens to their story of losing the friend they thought might be the Messiah, and the rumors of his resurrection, Jesus responds by interpreting the scriptures for them (verse 27).

After hearing Jessica's story, the catechist helps her to link her experience and her religious heritage: What does scripture have to say about that? For instance, "How do you show anger? forgiveness?" leads into "How did Jesus show anger? forgiveness?"

Children experiencing the challenges and delights of friendship may want to learn about Jesus and his friends: Mary, Martha, Lazarus, Peter, John and the other disciples. Children feeling rejected should know about Jesus' welcome to all people, even the socially excluded ones, and his own betrayal by Judas.

In other words, we help Jessica see her personal stories in light of the gospel story. We bring the lens of our religious tradition to bear on her concerns, making the connection between two equally important components of the process.

Invite Action

The disciples in the Emmaus story take two kinds of action. First, their encounter with the hungry, homeless stranger on the road late in the day leads to an offer of hospitality. Central to the Christian life is that impulse to offer food and shelter for the night, the movement from knowledge to action.

Second, despite the fact that they had just completed an arduous, seven-mile walk to Emmaus, the disciples' recognition of the risen Lord energizes them so much that they immediately retrace their steps. They walk the seven miles back to Jerusalem because they are anxious to share good news. "They told what had happened on the road, and how he had been made known to them in the breaking of the bread" (verse 35).

Thus, the reading of scripture is an impetus to action. After hearing the gospel, ask:
• What does this gospel call us to do?

Try to keep the discussion of action concrete and practical. Without being a "wet blanket," steer the children toward activity that is within their realm of possibility. Thus, eliminating world hunger, while a worthy goal, is beyond the limitations of most individuals. However, a group commitment to work one afternoon at the Catholic Worker soup kitchen is doable.

Remember also that the world of most children, while narrow, still needs their efforts. Helping a younger child with homework may not sound earth-shaking, but is a valid form of Christian action. If children are unable to work in the larger realm of social action, encourage them to find ways of living out the gospel in their homes, schools, parishes and neighborhoods.

Celebrate the Faith

The disciples finally recognized Jesus when he took bread, blessed and broke it (verse 30). Thus, they knew him through a familiar, ritual action. The final step, then, is to ask: How does what we have read and discussed lead us to ritual action or prayer? Search out the symbols, images and ritual actions that are present in the scriptures or spring from them. Use these for the prayer service that concludes the session.

Sample Session with Children: Family Issues

This sample session begins with a common family problem: sibling conflict. Sibling problems aren't new: consider Cain and Abel, Joseph and his brothers, Jacob and Esau, Rachel and Leah. These stories should reassure participants that problems with siblings are normal. Jealousy is justified, but physical violence never is. God acts in the context of sibling relationships, even through struggles, and gives us siblings as companions and friends.

This sample uses the parable of the prodigal son, Luke 15:11-32, the Gospel for the Twenty-Fourth Sunday in Ordinary Time, Year C. In the story, Jesus describes God as a merciful father who loves each child despite his flaws.

TIP: Getting Started
A tour of the church is appropriate for this period. Encourage the children to ask questions about everything they find there. Include "backstage" areas such as the sacristy and inside the confessionals.

The sample can serve as a model to design other sessions based on the specific life issues that concern children in your group. Note the progression in activities:

- An ice-breaker activity invites participants to discuss their own family situations.
- Discussion leads into the story from scripture.
- Reflection on the scripture invites action.
- The session culminates in prayer.

Opening Activity

Before the session begins: On slips of paper or index cards, briefly describe situations of conflict between siblings. Adapt these to the ages of participants. You may use the suggestions of children in your group, or the following examples:

- Two siblings argue about who will feed the dog or cat, take out the trash, play with a younger sibling, etc.
- Two step-siblings fight over which TV program to watch, when both have favorites on different channels at the same time.
- Older siblings discuss curfews, allowances, restrictions on dating, drinking or use of the car.

Number the slips of paper so that two of them are #1, two are #2, etc. Place them in a basket and invite each person to draw a slip. Then ask group members to find the partner with the paper numbered the same as theirs. Explain:

- Your partner is your brother or sister. You don't get along too well.
- You're about to have an argument over a typical problem.

Invite one pair to roleplay the conflict described on the paper. After two or three minutes, stop the roleplay and ask:

- Who can relate to this situation? How?
- How would this problem have played out at your house?

Repeat the activity and discussion with each pair until all have had a turn. Then say: Let's look at a story in scripture that shows sibling conflict and a very special father.

Scripture: Luke 15:11-32

You may present the story in various ways. You may ask several group or team members to prepare in advance to act it out. You may ask different people to read different parts. You may even transpose the story into a popular television setting. After the story is read or dramatized, discuss:

- What did you hear in this story?
- What kind of person is the younger son? Include his good points and his faults.
- Who in your family is most like this son?
- Repeat the questions for the older son and father.
- How does the father handle the conflict?
- What do you think the father wanted for his two sons?
- In what ways are your family fights like the one in Jesus' story? Are your solutions similar?
- In your family or at school, are you ever like the father?
- How do you think Jesus would tell the story if it was about you?

Action

Throughout the discussion, consider what action may arise from today's session. Invite participants to respond to these ques-

tions by discussing them with a partner or small group, or by writing their answers on an index card or journal, or by drawing their response:
- What is the one thing you remember most from today's session?
- As a result of today's session, what is one thing you will do differently this week when you fight with a sibling?
- What is one positive thing you could do for a brother, sister or parent—before a fight even gets started? What is one concrete way you could show the attitude of the father in the Bible story?

Prayer
- Ask the children to sit quietly in a circle or in small groups. Invite them to name the places where they want to act like the merciful Father.
- When there is quiet, have them repeat the Prayer of St. Francis after you. Also have copies available for them to take home.

> Lord, make me an instrument of
>   your peace:
> where there is hatred, let me sow
>   love;
> where there is injury, pardon;
> where there is despair, hope;
> where there is darkness, light;
> and where there is sadness, joy.
>
> O Divine Master, grant that I may not so much seek to be consoled as to console, to be understood as to understand, to be loved as to love.
>
> For it is in giving that we receive, it is in pardoning that we are pardoned, and it is in dying that we are born to eternal life.

Encourage the children to use the prayer during the week or when they have problems at home. Encourage the parents to use the prayer, too, and to praise the children's efforts to act mercifully.

On copies of the Prayer of St. Francis, you could add the father's words from scripture and encourage the parents to pray these over their children at bedtime, using their child's name:
- "(*Name*), you are always with me, and all that is mine is yours."

Sample Family Session: Power Over/Power With

At least once a month and perhaps more often, gather families together. The wide range of ages can present a challenge. The following session is structured to encourage everyone's participation.

This sample session is based on a problem common to many families: bullies. Bullies come in many shapes and sizes. They run the gamut from the child who steals lunch money to a tyrannical teacher or an arrogant sibling. They can be verbally abusive or as violent as the gang leaders who bully with guns.

Begin by asking participants to describe, to a small group or a partner, their experience with bullies. For adults this may prompt a childhood memory or a more recent time of working for a mean boss. The groups or partners should simply listen to the descriptions, not trying to "fix" the situations or give advice. Stress that the role people should play for each other is that of the empathetic listener.

Encourage the children to use the prayer of St. Francis during the week or when they have problems at home.

They may also try to find common themes in their stories: for instance, bullies abuse power. If you wish, you may broaden your discussion to the misuse of power, but try to keep it concrete and specific.

A variety of scriptures describe confrontations with bullies:

> David and Goliath (1 Samuel 17:19-51)
> Jesus and the devil (Matthew 4:1-11; Luke 4:1-13)
> Jesus confronts the Pharisees about the woman taken in adultery (John 8:1-12)

This sample session uses the gospels for the Feast of Christ the King. You could also use the story of the Good Shepherd (John 10:1-18). In these gospels, Jesus models a different use of power: not over people, but with people. He rejects violence and praises service.

Year A — Matthew 25:31-46
God rewards simple service, such as giving a drink of water. When we help those who need us, we find God in them.

Year B — John 18:33-37
Jesus rejects earthly kingship or power. His followers do not fight to defend him because his kingdom is not of this world.

Year C — Luke 23:35-43
As the people jeer him, Jesus gives his kingdom to a thief.

As you probe one of these scriptures, remind participants that Jesus is our King and invites us to be kings and queens with him forever. This is a wonderful way to affirm a child. If we believe that Christ made us royal as he was, we don't need to bully

Remind participants that Jesus is our King and invites us to be kings and queens with him forever. This is a wonderful way to affirm a child.

anyone. We act nonviolently and compassionately, as Christ did. We also have an inner strength to resist bullies, and an understanding of their insecurity. If you have time, continue your discussion during one of the following activities:

Option 1:
Give children power as they take turns being king or queen. Give the royalty a special throne, a crown made from foil or construction paper, perhaps a cape from the thrift shop, drama closet or dress-up box.

After all have had a turn, discuss:
• How do people treat royalty?
• What power do you have as royalty that you wouldn't otherwise have?
• What would you do for your people if you were king or queen?
• How is Jesus different from the other kind of royalty we've talked about?
• What does Jesus do for his people?
• What does this mean for us who want to be like him?

Imagining that you are royal, create a decree, using elaborate language and decorations. For example: I, Queen Maria, do hereby decree that every subject in my royal realm devour a royal ice-cream sundae every day and twice on Saturdays.

Then create a decree that Jesus might issue.
• How would his decree be different from a bully's decree?

Option 2:
Prepare to dramatize the story of the orphaned princess (below) for younger members of the group or for children in the parish nursery or day care center. Optional props:

- crowns for the king and queen
- pig ears, faces or snouts
- a wig and cane for the old woman
- a shovel and potatoes for the princess

When a king and queen knew that foreign invasion was imminent and their family would be killed, they preserved their daughter's life by sending her to live anonymously with a pig farmer. The child grew up unaware of her royal lineage until one day an old woman, who knew the truth, whispered, "You are the daughter of the most high king." After that, the orphaned princess still dug potatoes and fed pigs but with a new dignity, a restored sense of her noble heritage.

Option 3:
Write the word *Christian* in large letters down the left side of newsprint or chalkboard. Then fill in words or phrases starting with each letter of the word, forming an acrostic. Let each word or phrase describe a compassionate follower of Jesus. For example:
- **C**ompassionate
- **H**umorous
- **R**esponsive to others' needs
- **I**nvolved
- **S**ecure inside
- **T**ruthful
- **I**nterested in everything
- **A**ctive
- **N**ever finished

Then divide into pairs. Give each pair one quality from the acrostic, but keep these secret. Each pair is to make a human sculpture of their word. One partner is the sculptor and the other, the clay. Invite the group to guess which quality the pair is portraying.

Option 4:
Prepare a royal feast for the whole group decorating the room for a banquet, hanging the decrees children made (above), providing "thrones," treats to eat and drink, other symbols of nobility such as capes and crowns.

Prayer Service
Conclude by having the parents anoint the children. Use the prayers for anointing found in chapter 5, "Minor Rites and Ritual Gestures." Make the connection between royalty and anointing. Remembering that Christ is King of Compassion, pray for those in need, mentioning them by name. Appropriate music might be "You Have Anointed Me," or "The King of Glory."

Notes
1. Kiersey, David and Marilyn Bates, *Please Understand Me* (Gnosology Books, 1984).

2. Frank Sokol and Maureen Kelly, *Preparing Children for the Sacraments of Christian Initiation* (St. Anthony Messenger Press, 1989), Audiocassette.

Prepare a royal feast for the whole group decorating the room for a banquet.

Chapter 7

Period of Catechumenate
(*RCIA*, #75–105)

For children's activities on the catechumenate, see initiation journals, pp. 12-17.

To help parents and sponsors understand the catechumenate, see the *Parent and Sponsor Guide*, pp. 22-26.

Jessica was excited after the rite of welcome. She and several others had waited nervously outside the church, then entered its warmth, a place filled with music, candlelight and people eager to welcome her. She cherished the memory of her mother signing the cross on her forehead, ears, eyes, lips, heart, shoulders, hands and feet. So she entered enthusiastically into the next period of initiation, the catechumenate.

Purpose of the Period

The purpose of this second period is to deepen faith by celebrating the rites, breaking open the scriptures and entering the community life of prayer and service. A gradual catechesis follows the liturgical year and gives a sense of the mysteries in which Christians participate. The emphasis is on Jessica's personal relationship with God, not simply her gaining information about God. She travels this journey of spiritual conversion with "suitable pastoral formation and guidance." Catechumens learn "in all things to keep their hopes set on Christ," (*RCIA*, #75.2), and to become more prayerful and loving, even at the cost of self-sacrifice. The inner transition should be shown by a change in outward behavior.

The length of this period depends on individual circumstances, but should be long enough (several years if necessary) for the child's faith to become strong.

Rites of the Catechumenate

The catechesis of this period flows into and from the rites. The catechumenate is marked by two threshold rites: the rite of acceptance or welcome and the rite of election.

The heart of catechumenal catechesis is formation through the word and the minor rites. This period calls for liturgical catechesis, the method based on the Sunday celebration of the word. It might be very different from what you have been used to as a Director of Religious Education. The children are ordinarily dismissed from Mass before the liturgy of the eucharist for this session. Every catechetical session includes:
• breaking open the word
• a blessing done by the catechist
• at times, minor exorcisms and anointings that flow from the scripture

"The Church, like a mother, helps the catechumens on their journey by means of suitable liturgical rites, which purify the catechumens little by little and strengthen them with God's blessing" (*RCIA*, #75.3). (See chapter 4 for more on these rites.)

In addition to celebrations of the word of God, the catechumenate also includes the minor exorcisms, the optional Ephphetha rite (*RCIA*, #197–199), the presentations of the Creed and the Lord's Prayer (*RCIA*, #79, #104–105). Or you may delay the latter presentations until the next period, purification and enlightenment. You will also

want to continue the prayer experiences and ritual gestures begun in the inquiry period, such as lighting a candle and joining hands for prayer (*RCIA*, #79-81). (See chapter 5, "Minor Rites and Ritual Gestures.")

Celebrations of the Word

(*RCIA*, #79, #81–89)
Using the Children's Lectionary may make the gospel easier for children who may be hearing it for the first time. By now, they should all have identical books of the gospels, so they can gain practical experience locating the passages. After participants proclaim the word or present it through storytelling or drama, catechists should explain difficult terms in contemporary language. Invite the children to put the message into their own framework: modern experiences, settings and words.

When possible introduce them to the customs of other countries, especially to all the ethnic traditions represented in your parish. For instance, invite them to show their respect for the word as people do in India. They sit with their hands resting on their knees, palms turned upwards, to show they want to receive God's gifts.

Provide a "Question Box" at each session for children who may be too shy to ask their questions aloud. Remind everyone that no question is stupid. From the celebrations of the word flows a commitment to service.

Service

The word forms people in an attitude of mission or service. Furthermore, the com-

This period calls for liturgical catechesis, the method based on the Sunday celebration of the word. It might be very different from what you have been used to as a Director of Religious Education.

**TIP: Talking with
Parents**

**Topics to cover with
parents as you meet
with them during this
period:**

- **The child's choice of
  a godparent. This
  should be made
  before the rite of
  election.**

- **Starting family
  rituals at home.
  Parents who are
  unchurched may not
  know how to say
  grace or introduce
  family ritual.
  Recommend the
  material in the
  *Parent and Sponsor
  Guide,* or a book of
  family prayers and
  rituals.**

munity models serving others in a variety of ways. Through this example, children learn that being a Christian involves a commitment to all God's people. Practical ways to include the service component are:

- Invite volunteers from different ministries to participate in sessions and explain their work. Emphasize the volunteer aspect.
- Help with hunger issues:
  — Invite a speaker and/or obtain a video from Bread for the World.[1]
  — Participate in parish programs such as Loaves and Fishes, supporting a soup kitchen or stocking a food bank. Emphasize those that help children their own age.
  — Encourage families to have a simple, meatless meal once a week and contribute the money saved to a program that alleviates hunger.
- Service in the domestic arena:
  — Mow lawns, shovel walks, weed gardens, baby-sit, walk neighbors' pets, help younger siblings with homework—without charge.
  — Arrange for classes at school, scout troop, athletic teams to collect trial-sized toiletries for a homeless shelter.
  — Have the same groups collect toys, puzzles, books, etc., for the children in a battered women's shelter.
  — Have families adopt a "grandparent," an elderly person who needs transportation to church, doctor appointments, etc., or would enjoy being included in family activities.
  — Have families "adopt" a high school or college-aged transfer student from another country who would like to share in family outings, meals, etc.
- Discuss with a small group or sponsor:
  — How can a person my age make a difference in someone else's life?

- Whom do you admire for their efforts to serve others? Why?
- Why is it so important to live a life of service?
- Have a "ministry scavenger hunt," prepared in advance, where older participants help younger children to find and briefly interview:
  — a founding member of the parish
  — a teenager who belongs to the youth group
  — a lector
  — a eucharistic minister
  — an artist, musician or singer
  — a person who works with the sick, elderly, dying or grieving members of the parish
  — a member of the St. Vincent de Paul or Knights of Columbus organization
  — a member of the medical profession
  — a social worker
- When they return from the "hunt," ask:
  — What is this person's ministry?
  — What does he or she like best about his or her ministry?
  — What's the one thing you'll remember about this person?

Sample Celebration of the Word of God: The Call to Discipleship

(*RCIA* #81–89)

The catechumens should celebrate the first part of the Sunday Mass, then be dismissed after the liturgy of the word. Together, they can then break open the word with their catechists. In some parishes, the catechetical session happens later in the week, perhaps in the evening. If this is the case, where this celebration does not occur in the context of a Sunday Mass, use the structure that follows.

A. Song

To follow the theme of the gospel, choose a song about discipleship and teach children the first verse or chorus, for example, "We Are Called, We Are Chosen."

B. Reading

There are many readings about the call to discipleship from which to choose, for example:
- the call of Abraham (Genesis 12:1-9)
- Samuel's calling (1 Samuel 3:1-21)
- the annunciation (Luke 1:26-38)
- the calling of Matthew (Luke 5:27-32)
- the Samaritan woman (John 4:1-42)

The following sample session uses the reading for the Third Sunday in Ordinary Time, Year A: Matthew 4:12-23.

C. Homily

The catechist should give a brief homily that explains and applies the readings, inviting the children's participation. After the song and the reading, ask the children:
- What did you hear?
- How are you called just as Andrew, Peter, James and John were called?
- What does this gospel call you to do?

Several kinds of content could emerge from the gospel and the group. If you have time for an activity, choose one or more of the following and continue your discussion of discipleship informally as you do it together.

Option 1: In Jesus' Shoes

Gather the group in a circle, or with a larger group in several small circles. Invite all group members but three to pile their shoes in the middle of the circle. Add to the pile three pairs of sandals.

Give everyone these directions:
- Take any two *mismatched* shoes from the pile.
- Don't take your own shoes.
- When I say *go*, start passing shoes to your left, as fast as you can.
- Hand shoes carefully; don't throw them. The purpose is not to get rid of the shoes, but to keep them moving.
- I'll tell you when to stop.

Say *go* and after about twenty seconds of shoe-passing, say *stop*. Ask:
- Who ended up with one of Jesus' shoes (the sandal)?
- If you did, put it on and tell us:
  — What does it mean to walk in Jesus' shoes? (Anticipate comments on care for people who seem lost, efforts at healing or reconciliation, appreciation of God's world, reverence for others.)
  — What's one way you can walk in Jesus' shoes this week?

Repeat the exercise several times, gathering different comments. Then say:
- How many of you think it would be hard to walk in Jesus' shoes? Why?
- What helped Jesus do all he did?
- What helps us act like him?

If possible, invite guests from the parish, members of the team, or those who were initiated last year to talk about how they try to follow Jesus, and what helps them to do so.

If possible, invite guests from the parish, members of the team, or those who were initiated last year to talk about how they try to follow Jesus, and what helps them to do so.

Today, God calls us to follow and serve Jesus. We all have different gifts and we are called to different tasks.

Option 2: Fishing for People

Invite the children to make a poster of people that we can catch for God. Ask them to cut fish shapes from assorted colors of construction paper or fold them from origami paper. Then, children draw peoples' pictures or cut faces from magazines and glue them onto the fish. (If a Polaroid camera is available, take pictures of the children in the group and add these.) Then attach pieces of mesh (from bags used for onions or oranges) or plastic mesh to resemble fish nets, over the pictures. As you work, discuss:

- Who did Jesus call to fish for people?
- How did Jesus want his friends to catch people?
- Who follows Jesus today? Who can we "catch" for Jesus? How do we do this?

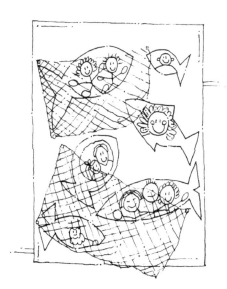

Option 3: "Why Me?"

Ask the question, "Why would God call me?" Explain that Peter, Andrew, James and John might have asked themselves the same question. Yet Jesus knew exactly what

he was doing when he called them. They had the special qualities they would need for the jobs God gave them to do.

Today, God calls us to follow and serve Jesus. We all have different gifts and we are called to different tasks. This activity helps us to name our talents and reflect on how we are called.

Distribute pencils and paper. Label the front and back of a paper (or 2 separate papers):
- I am unique. (Use the word "special" for younger children.)
- God calls me.

Ask the children to complete the two lists. On the first, they should list special things about themselves which make them feel pleased. Some may be when they were younger, like learning to ride a bike. Some may be recent, like playing the guitar or helping with younger children.

On the second list, they can write or draw several things God has called them to do in the past, or may be calling them to do today. The first list of gifts and talents may help them understand what God may be calling them to do. For instance, skill at art may lead to sharing this ability with others: designing cards for the sick, posters for home, school or church.

Option 4: Letters of Recommendation

Suggest that because Jesus had so much confidence in his first followers, they were able to do things they never thought possible. Jesus himself drew strength from the Father who said, "This is my Son, the Beloved, with whom I am well pleased." With a partner (either a sponsor or peer companion) talk about times you felt "down" on yourself: dumb, klutzy, unable to do much.

- What does the support of a friend, coach, teacher or parent mean at a time like that?
- How has your self-image been bolstered by another person's positive comments about you?
- How do you think the first disciples felt about themselves when they heard, "you [will] fish for people" (Mt. 4:19)?
- Imagine God saying to you, "This is my beloved daughter or son, with whom I am well pleased." How does that feel? How might it affect your life at home? at school? with friends?

Provide writing paper and pens or pencils. Ask each partner to write a letter of recommendation for the other. Write as if you were recommending this person for friendship with another friend. Include the partner's good qualities. If the partners don't know each other well, they should spend some time getting acquainted. Conclude by reading each other the letters and giving them to each other.

D. Concluding Rite: Minor Exorcism

With hands outstretched over the catechumens, the catechist says the following prayer (*RCIA* #94, F). Prayers H, I and J also tie in with discipleship. The wording of all the prayers may be adapted for children. The prayer may also be followed by an anointing or laying on of hands to stress that each child is called by Christ to discipleship.

Lord and God,
you know the secrets of our hearts
and reward us for the good we do.

Look kindly on the efforts and progress
   of your [children].
Strengthen them on their way,
increase their faith,
and accept their repentance.
Open them to your goodness and justice
and lead them to share in your sacraments on earth,
until they finally enjoy your presence in heaven.

We ask this through Christ our Lord.
Amen.

Prayer

In the week after the session, children may want to pray at home about being disciples. Alert the parents that this has been the focus of their session, and that children may want to continue to discuss discipleship and pray about it. Give them these sentence completion prayers to get them started on silent prayer, or a written or artistic response.

- Jesus, you are calling me right now. (Pause.)
- Jesus, one of the things I think you are calling me to do is...(Pause.)
- To do this for you, I must take a risk. That's hard. I'll need you to help me... (Pause.)
- Jesus, for me the scariest thing about following you is...(Pause.)
- Jesus, the neatest thing about following you is...(Pause.)
- Jesus, thank you for calling me to follow you. *Amen.*

Prayer may be followed by an anointing or laying on of hands to stress that each child is called by Christ to discipleship.

Sample Family Session: Epiphany

The family session should be preceded by a Sunday assembly, from which the group is dismissed to break open the word. If the session does not occur in this context (because it is held later during the week), structure it with:

    A. Song
    B. Reading
    C. Homily
    D. Concluding rite

The readings for this feast are the same in Years A, B and C:

    Isaiah 60:1-6
    Psalm 72:1-2, 7-8, 10-13
    Ephesians 3:2-3, 5-6
    Matthew 2:1-12

Central Questions

Explore all together, or with smaller groups, the central questions raised by this feast.

Explore all together, or with smaller groups, the central questions raised by this feast:

- What does *epiphany* mean? (commonly used to mean a flash of insight; to the church, Epiphany means the revealing of Jesus as the Christ to the Gentiles)
- What "epiphanies" or sudden moments of clarity or insight have we experienced?
- What dark forces in our world correspond to Herod's murderous armies?
- What are the "stars" that guide us?
- What prevents us from being open to the gifts of other people, especially those who are different?
- What practical ways have we found to be more open to these unexpected gifts?

Options

Depending on the time available, choose one or more activities from the following options:

- Read *The Three Wise Kings* by Tomie de Paola.
- Make a mural illustrating the journey of the kings, with the crèche at one end. Decorate the kings with gift wrap, glitter, crayons or markers. Draw the places through which they passed.
- Dramatize the gospel, asking volunteers to take the parts of the narrator, the visitors from the East, King Herod and the prophet Micah, quoted in verse 6.
- Make luminarias for the final prayer service or to take home; use paper bags, sand, small candles and scissors to cut designs in the bag. Each child cuts designs such as small stars in his or her own bag, then weights the bag with sand and inserts an unlit candle. When used for the prayer service, dim lights in the room and light the candles with a long taper.
- Design a banner, centered on today's scripture passages, to be used for Mass on the Feast of Epiphany 20 years from now. Ask the church historian to store it in a "time capsule" with other church memorabilia. As the participants make the banner, encourage them to speculate on how they might be different and how Mass might be different by then. It will be the *children's* responsibility to remember to use it!
- Discuss attitudes toward other religions and the practice of **ecumenism,*** in light of today's revelation to *all* people.[2] This may be especially helpful if group members are coming to the Catholic Church from other denominations, and/or still

have close friends and family members in other traditions. What challenges does this pose? What blessings does it bring?

- Explain the Epiphany custom of blessing the house, a symbol that the home is holy ground. How is the kitchen sacred space? the bathroom? Suggest that people carry a lit candle through the house, with different family members taking turns blessing each room. Or provide small pieces of chalk for the Epiphany custom of marking the front door with a cross.

Prayer Service

The concluding prayer service includes a blessing. You may also use the dramatization of the gospel and/or the luminarias prepared by the group.

Blessing Rite (RCIA, #95-97)

Children who are candidates and catechumens should form a circle with their companions or sponsors facing them. The companion or sponsor then extends hands over the child and prays (*RCIA #97* I):

Lord,
look with love on your [children],
who commit themselves to your name
and bow before you in worship.

Help them to accomplish what is good;
arouse their hearts,
that they may always remember your
      works and your commands
and eagerly embrace all that is yours.
Grant this through Christ our Lord.
      Amen.

End with an Epiphany song such as "We Three Kings of Orient Are,""Lord Today," or "Arise, Shine."

Luminarias and songs enhance the closing prayer services.

Notes

1. Bread for the World, 802 Rhode Island Ave. N.E., Washington, D.C. 20018, (202) 269-0200.

2. For background, see *Vatican Council II: The Conciliar and Post Conciliar Documents*, "Directory Concerning Ecumenical Matters: Part One" and "Declaration on the Relation of the Church to Non-Christian Religions" (Collegeville MN: Liturgical Press, 1975), 483 and 743.

Period of Purification and Enlightenment
(*RCIA*, #138–149)

Purpose of the Period

For children's activities on purification and enlightenment, see initiation journals, pp. 22-30.

To help parents and sponsors understand purification and enlightenment, see the *Parent and Sponsor Guide*, pp. 27-30.

This period usually coincides with Lent and is a time of preparation for the celebration of the paschal mystery. It is a time more of spiritual preparation than of catechetical instruction, focused on a deepening knowledge of Christ. The theme of repentance is expressed through Lenten **scrutinies*** or penitential rites (*RCIA*, #291–294).

"We need to translate the jargon of the paschal mystery into events in the lives of families. If sacraments are not things or empty rituals but actions of people who die

and rise today and who bring that to eucharist, where do families die and rise?"
—*James Dunning*[1]

The answers to the question Dunning raises are as close at hand as the people in our groups. Jessica knew the sorrow of her grandmother's death, failures at school and arguments with even her best friend Lupe. During this period, she learned that she did not suffer alone. Her sadness is joined to that of the community and to the passion of Christ.

In the parish community, families die when their jobs are threatened or taken away.

They die when there is illness, death, emotional or physical violence in the home. They die when a parent walks out or a relationship is broken. Younger members are affected when teenagers experience unplanned pregnancies, drug or alcohol addictions and failures in school. Children baptized into Christ are also baptized into his death.

Rene, Chris and Daniel, siblings in Rita Burns Senseman's initiation group, came from a single-parent, inner-city home with six children and four grandchildren. Problems with their older brothers and sister often caused havoc in the household. Their mother was often tired or upset, yet they could see how she held the family together. In her strength, they "came to see...the power and promise of the paschal mystery."[2]

Just as the birth of a baby in a family brings the joy of new life, so children bring to the church the gifts of energy, hope, spontaneous affection and blindness to human failings. As they enter into the paschal mystery, they can identify, in a variety of ways including art, roleplay, mime, etc., where they find death and new life in their own experience. For as they are baptized into Christ, they are also participants in his glorious resurrection.

See chapters 4 and 5 for the rites of this period:
- Lenten ritual (chap. 5)
- Penitential rites—scrutinies (chap. 4)
- Presentation of the Creed and the Lord's Prayer (chap. 5)

Traditional Practices

Lent originated as a pre-baptismal retreat, a period of intensified prayer, fasting and almsgiving to prepare for the sacraments of initiation. It is a good time to introduce these traditional practices in ways with which the children can connect.

Prayer

- Arrange for the participants in your group to be "prayer partners" for a week or throughout Lent. This could include:
  — praying for each other's intentions
  — phoning or writing a note to encourage each other
  — being partners for activities such as breaking open the word
- Introduce, if you haven't already, the concept of prayer as "listening." Encourage children to sit in silence with God. Begin with only one to two minutes; extend the time if the children wish.
- Pray with a focal point, such as a cross, a candle, a special picture or statue, and/or soft background music.
- Pray over a scripture passage. You may:
  — concentrate on one phrase from the passage, memorize it or repeat it to yourself, such as: "Little children, you are from God..." (1 John 4:4) or "Everyone who loves is born of God and knows God" (1 John 4:7).
  — imagine yourself in the scene: What do you hear? smell? taste? see? touch?
  — write a journal entry as if you had been a character in the passage. For instance, one boy wrote, "Today I went with Jesus to the Garden. He asked me to pray with him, but I kept falling asleep..."
  — illustrate the scene in scripture.

Just as the birth of a baby in a family brings the joy of new life, so children bring to the church the gifts of energy, hope, spontaneous affection and blindness to human failings.

• Introduce a guided meditation by reading a scripture passage, pausing after every verse to allow children to enter the story. Invite them to close their eyes as you insert questions such as these:
— Who is standing beside you?
— What are you feeling? What questions do you have?
— What do you say to Jesus?
— What does Jesus say to you?

Remind children not to answer these questions aloud, but to imagine their responses silently.

Fasting

A typical Lenten practice is to eat less or simpler food and to give the poor the money saved. A Lenten tradition for many Catholic children is Operation Rice Bowl.[3] Another way to fast is to discuss with children:

• How would you most like to live?
• What keeps you from living like that?
• What opportunities do you have at school, at home, in your neighborhood to act like Christ? (For example, befriending the child no one likes.)
• What behaviors do you want to keep? Which ones do you want to move beyond?
• How can we help each other live the way we most want to?

Almsgiving

While you may want to ask children to help collect money or food for the poor, or participate in a parish effort, they may benefit more from service that brings them into more direct contact with those in need. This breaks down the barriers between brothers and sisters in the Body of Christ and helps

them see that need isn't always a matter of money. They may already be engaged in such work. If so, this is a time to intensify their commitment and to share what they have learned.

These forms of outreach ask for time in Lent:

• Brainstorm a list of people in the parish or neighborhood who could use a little kindness. Write each name on a piece of paper, mix them in a hat and have each child draw a name. They then make a card or write a note to the person whose name they have drawn. Provide addresses from the parish directory, and mail the notes.

• Have each person decide on a sacrifice he or she could make for one family member this week. (For example, "I'll get up in the morning the first time mom calls me," or "I'll read a bedtime story to my little sister three nights this week.") Each writes the commitment on a piece of paper and puts it in a stamped, self-addressed envelope. Mail these to group members as mid-week reminders.

• Ask group members to think of one person they have wronged and take an action to correct the mistake. (For example, apologize, replace something broken, fix a problem.)

Key Symbols — Water, Light, Life

Through the Lenten scriptures, the children will become familiar with the symbols that also permeate the Easter Vigil. While they may begin to discuss their meaning now, they will fully "break open" the symbols after they have experienced them in the

TIP: Links to Parish Lenten Activities

Ask the social concerns committee, parish school and/or religious education director to include the children preparing for initiation in any Lenten activities they may be sponsoring, such as a Seder meal.

sacraments of initiation. The readings for Year A are used in connection with the scrutinies. Some people like to use the Hebrew Scriptures in preparation for the scrutiny, the gospel afterward. The gospels treat three interwoven levels of disorder in human life: personal (the Samaritan woman), social (the man born blind), and cosmic (Lazarus's death). They reveal three faces of God: the living water, the light of the world, the resurrection and the life.

First Scrutiny: Water
Exodus 17:3-7; John 4:5-42
(Third Sunday of Lent)

Before the scrutiny, read the Exodus passage and discuss:

- Moses' people grumbled because they were so thirsty. Sometimes we thirst for more than a drink.
  — What do you thirst for or long for?
  — What do you think the world thirsts for or needs most?

If possible, arrange with the parish liturgist to have the children's responses included in the scrutiny prayers.

Activities based on the symbol of water:
As time allows, choose one of the following activities and continue your discussion of water during the activity.

- To experience directly the life-giving power of water, give each child a heavy paper cup, a packet of sugar, a packet of yeast and a coffee stirrer. Have them stir the sugar into a cup half-filled with water. Then sprinkle a little yeast over the top of the water. Watch for signs of life: bubbles, froth, etc.
- Give each child a shallow paper bowl filled with potting soil. Plant bean seeds

in the bowl, then sprinkle grass seed on top of the soil. Spray with water or place an ice cube on top. Have children take the gardens home, asking: What will your garden need daily to sprout? (water) Point out that just as yeast and grass cannot grow without water, so people need it.

- Make a poster of the ways people use water. Tear a cloud shape from blue or gray paper. Glue it to poster board. Then ask each child to draw on paper, shaped like a water droplet, one way that people use water.

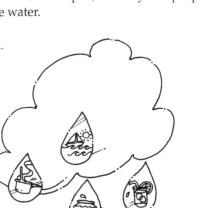

- After hearing the gospel, ask:
  — How are Jesus and the woman using the word *water* in two different ways? (Children may not grasp the full meaning of his metaphor, but can see several differences: Jesus' water cannot be seen or touched, it does not run out, etc.)
  — What do you long for Jesus to give you? your family? the world?
- Divide into several groups and ask each one to make a comic strip poster, showing the gospel story in four panels.

"The water that I will give will become in them a spring of water gushing up to eternal life."
—*John 4:14*

"We must work the works of him who sent me while it is day... I am the light of the world."

—John 9:4-5

Second Scrutiny: Light
1 Samuel 16:1, 6-7, 10-13; John 9:1-41
(Fourth Sunday of Lent)

Before the scrutiny, read the passage from 1 Samuel and ask:

• What did the Lord help Samuel to see?
• What do you want God to help you see?
• What do you think other people sometimes fail to see? Where do we all need help seeing?

If possible, arrange with the parish liturgist to have the children's responses included in the scrutiny prayers.

Activities based on the symbol of light:

• Discuss experiences of fearing the dark. Ask:
  — Why do many people fear the dark?
  — Why do people usually prefer the light?
• After proclaiming the gospel, have a few volunteers act as Jesus, the disciples, the healed man and the neighbors. Invite the others to interview them. Sample questions:
  — Healed man, how will your life change now that you can see?
  — Jesus, what do you want the healed man to do next?
  — Disciple, were you surprised? Why or why not?
  — Neighbor, what do you think about Jesus?
• Ask children to cut symbols of light, such as flashlights, candles, light bulbs, etc., from construction paper. On their shape, have them write one way they can bring light this week. Invite them to take their shape home as a reminder.
• Conclude with a prayer service in a dark room, where the group gathers around lighted candles. Ask:

— How is God like light?
• Ask group members to reflect silently on a place in their lives that feels dark, then to silently ask Jesus to bring his light into that place.
• Pray aloud together: "I am the light of the world. Whoever follows me will never walk in darkness" (John 8:12). Conclude by having each person turn to the one on his or her right, saying, "*(Name)*, I see God's light in you."

Third Scrutiny: Life and Death
Ezekiel 37:12-14; John 11:1-45
(Fifth Sunday of Lent)

Before the scrutiny, read the passage from Ezekiel and ask:

• Are there any places where you feel dead or hurt and need God to bring life?
• Where in our world do you see the need for God to bring life?

If possible, arrange with the parish liturgist to have the children's responses included in the scrutiny prayers.

Activities based on life and death:

• Begin by inviting each person to name an experience of loss. Although they may not yet have gone through the death of a beloved person, they may be able to talk about a pet dying or a friend moving away. Discuss:
  — How did it feel to go through this loss?
  — The feeling we have is called *grief.* What are some good ways to deal with grief? What ways of handling it are not so good?

You may want to continue by having them write brief letters to whomever or whatever they have lost. Or alert their parents that they may want to do this activity at home.

- You may want to prompt discussion by reading parts of a children's book on death, such as, *A Father Like That* by Charlotte Zolotow, *A Taste of Blackberries* by Doris Smith, *Today My Sister Died* by Ronee Domske, *Bridge to Terabithia* by Katherine Paterson, or *The Tenth Good Thing About Barney* by Judith Viorst. Select one suitable for the ages of the children, or have them read one at home.

- After proclaiming the gospel, divide the group into pairs to roleplay situations such as these:
  — Mary and Martha fret over Jesus' delay.
  — Martha tells Jesus about Lazarus's death.
  — Lazarus speaks to Mary after he has been raised from the dead.
  — Martha and Mary thank Jesus for bringing their brother back to life.

- Conclude with a prayer service:
  — Tell Jesus silently what worries you most about death.
  — Ask Jesus silently what you most want to know about life and death.
  — Pray aloud: "Jesus, you came to your friends when they needed you. Be with us too when we need you most. *Amen.*"

Sample Purification and Enlightenment Session: Passion (Palm) Sunday

This preparation for Holy Week is suitable for Passion Sunday. You may want to expand this session into a morning or day of retreat in preparation for Easter. Reading the entire passion story may be too long for some children. Instead, it may be more meaningful to select only a few sections of the story and to provide activities so that the children can enter into the shorter segments.

Gospels for Passion (Palm) Sunday:

Year A: Matthew 26:14–27:66
Year B: Mark 14:1–15:47
Year C: Luke 22:14–23:56

Option 1:

Divide into small groups and have each make a poster illustrating part of the passion. An adult or older child can read this section to the group before they make the poster. This sequence works for seven groups. With fewer children, eliminate some or ask groups to make two or more posters.

- Jesus rides into Jerusalem
- The Last Supper
- Garden of Gethsemane
- Jesus' trial
- Crucifixion
- Burial
- Resurrected Jesus meets Mary in the garden

Hang the posters on the wall in sequence. Then have the whole group walk together from one to the next as a leader tells the story.

Option 2:

Begin by making "props" to accompany a reading of Mark's gospel for Passion Sunday. Divide into small groups, each to make one of the following:

- chain from paper clips linked together
- sponge tied onto a stick

"I am the resurrection and the life. Those who believe in me, even though they die, will live, and everyone who lives and believes in me will never die. Do you believe this?"
—*John 11:25-26*

- sign: "King of the Jews" lettered onto an index card
- crown of thorns, braided from three pipe cleaners and formed into a circle
- whip: lengths of brown twine tied to a stick
- clock faces on three index cards, one showing 9:00, one 12:00, one 3:00.

Through the Ephphetha rite, the community symbolically opens the eyes and ears of those who will be initiated.

Place all these items in a paper bag, along with a small square of purple cloth, a stone, a cross and a pair of dice. Empty the contents of the bag on a table. Have the children remove the item as it is mentioned in the story. The references are from Mark 15: chain (v. 1), whip (v. 15), crown of thorns (v. 17), purple (v. 17), cross (v. 21), dice (v. 24), clock faces (vv. 25, 33-34), sign (v. 26), sponge (v. 36), stick (v. 36), stone (v. 46), empty bag (16:6). As the story ends, explain that the bag is empty just as Jesus' tomb is empty. The tomb could not hold Jesus. He rose again.

Review the story by having the children place the items back in the bag, then withdrawing them one at a time and telling what part each object played in the story.

Option 3:
Prepare a Way of the Cross for the whole group. Assign several stations to each person (depending on the numbers of your group). Ask them to read the name of the station, then to interpret that station in light of personal experience. For example, at the second station, Keesha says, "Jesus takes up his cross. I'm always fighting a problem with my weight. If I take up this cross as Jesus did, I don't feel so embarrassed and overwhelmed. It becomes a challenge to seize, as he did." (See "A Way of the Cross for Teens."[4])

Between stations, they may want to sing a traditional hymn such as "Stabat Mater" or "Were You There When They Crucified my Lord?"

Option 4:
Make Holy Week calendars to remember the days of Jesus' passion, death and resurrection.
- Give each person seven index cards, punch a hole in the same corner of each card and use ribbon to bind the cards together.
- On the front of the card, write what special feast we commemorate: for example, Holy Thursday, commemoration of the last supper (Jesus' giving the eucharist, washing feet); Good Friday, Jesus' crucifixion.
- On the back of the card, write or draw an activity to do that day: for example, Holy Thursday—bake bread.
- Encourage the children to share the calendars with their families. If you wish, list the times when services will be held at your parish, and arrange for the group to attend them together.

Ephphetha Rite
(*RCIA*, #197–199)
This rite is celebrated in preparation for the Easter Vigil, usually on Easter Saturday morning, often in the context of a retreat day. Ephphetha means "be opened!" The story of Jesus' curing the man who could not hear or speak (Mark 7:31-37) could be read or dramatized as part of this rite.

Through the rite, the community symbolically opens the eyes and ears of those who will be initiated: "that they may hear the word of God and profess it for their salvation" (*RCIA*, #197).

The presider touches the ears and lips of the children and says, "Ephphetha: that is, be opened, that you may profess the faith you hear, to the praise and glory of God."

Preparation for Triduum*

With a parent, sponsor or small group, discuss:
- Name a place that is special to you.
- What people do you associate with that place? (For example, a garden/my grandma)
- How do you remember someone dear who has died or moved away?

Using the responses to these questions, explain how the early Christians wanted to remember the last days of Jesus' life. They commemorated the final events in special places such as the upper room, the garden of Gethsemane, Calvary and the place of his burial. Without over-explaining, be sure that the child understands the significance of the following:
- Holy Thursday—commemorating the last supper and Jesus washing the feet of his disciples
- Good Friday—commemorating the crucifixion and burial of Jesus
- Holy Saturday—celebrating Jesus' resurrection from the dead

Keep in mind that the terminology we take for granted may be new to the children. Startled by the story of the crucifixion, Zach asked in amazement, "So why do you call it *Good* Friday?" His catechist responded, "I wonder about that too. I like a line from a poem: 'in spite of that, we call this Friday good.'[5]" Later the catechist explained, "I don't give a fig if Zach understands T.S. Eliot. I'm just introducing him to the company of his peers!"

Notes

1. James Dunning, "Let the Children Come to Me," ed. Victoria Tufano, *Readings in the Christian Initiation of Children* (Chicago: Liturgy Training Publications, 1994), 17.

2. Rita Burns Senseman, "What Should We Ask of Child Catechumens?" ed. Tufano, *Readings*, 156-157.

3. Operation Rice Bowl, c/o Catholic Relief Services, 209 W. Fayette St., Baltimore, MD 21201-3443, 1-800-222-0025.

4. Patti Normile, "A Way of the Cross for Teens," *Youth Update* (St. Anthony Messenger Press, 1989.)

5. T. S. Eliot, "Four Quartets," in *Collected Poems* (New York: Harcourt Brace, 1963), 188.

For information about prayer during this period of purification and enlightenment see the *Parent and Sponsor Guide*, pp. 52-56.

Chapter 9

Period of Mystagogy
(*RCIA*, #244–251)

For children's activities on mystagogy, see initiation journals, pp. 31-40.

To help parents and sponsors understand mystagogy, see the *Parent and Sponsor Guide*, pp. 31-35.

Jessica would always remember the Easter Vigil: the blaze in the night, the procession of candles, the surprise of the warm water, the perfumed oil, her first eucharist, the welcoming hugs from the people of her parish. She wanted time to think about what it had meant. That is the purpose of the final period, mystagogy, looking back in order to move forward.

After the resurrection, the gospels show befuddled disciples trying to understand what has happened to them. That reflective process takes time. Hence, mystagogy extends through the fifty days of Easter to Pentecost, then for a full year until the anniversary of initiation the following Easter.

In the early church when becoming Christian could be dangerous, some of the rituals were kept secret until after full initiation. During mystagogy, these secrets were revealed. But another meaning of "mystery" is sacrament: not as something we "get" but as an experience of God. During mystagogy we ponder the experience of the Holy through the initiation sacraments. "No one can truly be touched by the presence of the Holy and not be changed in some way. Mystagogy helps us give a name and some meaning to that change."[1] It means seeing things in new ways, through the lens of Christ's disciple.

Everything in mystagogy relates to the eucharist. All activities are oriented towards coming to the table each Sunday. During this time the neophytes meet monthly to break open the word. They continue their service projects, their deepening relationship to the community, and their growth in a life of prayer. While the Easter Vigil may have represented an emotional "high," or mountaintop experience, they learn to live on the plains of every day. The Christian life is not always a matter of "good feelings"; the new Christian must also move out of the spotlight and into ordinary time. Then, God's ever-present grace can make even the routine a source of deep joy.

Purpose of the Period

- to grow in a grasp of the paschal mystery
- to meditate on the gospel
- to share in the eucharist
- to do works of charity (*RCIA*, #244)

The initial welcome of the community that embraced the neophytes becomes a closer tie as the neophytes bring inspiration and energy to the community. Their weekly time of celebration together is the Sunday Mass of the Easter season, at which the neophytes and their godparents should have special reserved places.

Reflection after the Easter Vigil

One of the most important tasks after Easter is breaking open the meaning of the Easter Vigil. The children will probably be

eager to talk about it, so allow plenty of time for them to process what happened.

If you want to structure the process more carefully, recreate part of the experience to help the children remember it all. (Some parishes videotape the Vigil as an aid to later reflection.) Invite the children to close their eyes as a leader proceeds chronologically through the service. Mention a phrase from each of the readings and rites, for example: *Light of Christ!*

Evoke the sensate detail by singing or playing lines of the music. The sense most closely allied to memory is smell, so if possible, use some of the perfumed oil or incense to recapture the fragrances.

Divide the rite into short sections; after reviewing each, allow a few moments of silence, then invite the children to open their eyes. Discuss:
- What did you hear, see, smell, touch, taste?
- What feelings did you have about:
  — the fire?
  — the procession?
  — the stories or readings?
  — the water?
  — the chrism or oil?
  — the eucharist?
- Did you have any questions then that we could talk about now?
- What part of the Easter Vigil was best for you?

Sample Mystagogy Session: Promises

The following session is based on John 20:19-31, the reading for the Second Sunday of Easter in all three years.

The neophytes now celebrate a unique blessing: the eucharist.

Invite the children to contribute ideas for domestic service, such as: babysitting, pet care, dishwashing, recycling, yard work, letter-writing to the sick or lonely.

Begin with a ritual, such as lighting the Easter candle. You may also want to teach the traditional Easter greeting:

> *Leader:* Alleluia! Christ is risen!
> *Children:* The Lord is risen indeed. Alleluia!

Story

Then invite the children to listen to a gospel story of doubt and worry. Present John 20:19-31 through storytelling, dramatization or reading aloud. To capture the mood of the disciples, you may want to darken the room and encircle the group with a paper chain representing the locked doors.

Afterward, use the following questions to review the story, adapting them to the needs of your group:

• What did you hear in this story?
• When does this story take place?
• Why are the doors locked?
• How do you think the disciples feel now that Jesus is dead?
• Who appears to them?
• Why does Jesus show them his hands and side?
• How do the disciples feel when they see him?
• In what ways does Jesus come to us now?

Action

Discuss with a partner or small group:

• How do you feel about the promises you have made to other people and kept?
• How do you feel about promises you failed to keep?
• What does Jesus show us about keeping promises?

Lead into a discussion of opportunities for service projects:

• What project would you like to do?
• What kind of commitment does this project require? (time? transportation? other resources?)

You may wish to invite representatives of the various ministries to attend and explain their work. It is also helpful if they can provide information for the parents on what such a commitment involves.

Also stress the abundant opportunities for service at home. They may seem less dramatic or glamorous, but they meet real needs. Invite the children to contribute ideas for domestic service, such as: babysitting, pet care, dishwashing, recycling, yard work, letter-writing to the sick or lonely. Ask the children to think about their particular area of service before the next meeting, and discuss it with their families.

To help make the commitment more tangible, you may wish to create or copy a certificate on which they write or draw the service project they will undertake. You may then ritualize the commitment by having the children place their papers in a basket on the altar during a prayer service.

Activities

Depending on the size and ages of your group, you may wish to divide so that younger members may work on the art project, the Easter garden, and older youth can discuss doubt and questions. Or, you may invite everyone to join in the intergenerational project described below, the Easter garden.

Alternate projects are an Easter candle, Easter card or Easter tree. During the art projects, encourage conversation on the recent Easter Vigil or the Easter feast. Whether you create an Easter garden, an Easter tree or an Easter candle, use it as the focal point for the final prayer.

Activity 1: Easter Garden
Materials
    discarded newspapers
    cardboard tubes
    masking tape
    paste (liquid starch, wallpaper paste or a
        mixture of flour and water)
    balloon

Explain to group members that an Easter garden shows the empty tomb, one or more angels, the risen Jesus and his friends, and the flowers or trees of the garden where he appeared to Mary.

Make papier-mâché figures by first making "skeletons." Shape people by using the cardboard tubes, newspaper and masking tape to form standing figures. Begin a tomb shape by blowing up a balloon.

Cover these skeletons with one-inch strips of newspaper dipped into paste. These figures need to dry thoroughly before being cut or painted, so you may want to continue them in your next session, or have group members take them home to finish them, then return them at your next session.

Once the skeletons are dry, cut away as much of the balloon shape as needed to make an empty tomb. It may then be mounted on cardboard and painted the color of stone. The papier-mâché figures

may also be painted and decorated with cloth scraps, yarn, pipe cleaners or felt pens. Use paint and scraps to add details such as trees, flowers or small animals.

Activity 2: Question Box
For older members of your group, doubt is developmentally appropriate, and this gospel offers an opportunity to air their questions. Help them to voice and explore doubts, explaining that many of their questions may not have definitive answers. Assure them that doubting is healthy, a sign of being alive spiritually and wanting to know God better.

Invite teenagers to write down any questions about God, the Bible, the Catholic Church or spiritual life that they want to discuss. For example:
- If God is good, why is there so much suffering in the world?
- Sometimes Mass is boring. Why do we have to go?

(You may want to structure this activity so that you and team members have adequate

Assure them that doubting is healthy, a sign of being alive spiritually and wanting to know God better.

For more information on dealing with doubts see the *Parent and Sponsor Guide* pp. 33-34.

One important purpose of this period is to break open the meaning of the sacraments that the children have recently received.

time to see the questions in advance, or you may want to arrange a later session with a priest for more complex questions.) Provide index cards and pens or pencils, and allow ample time for everyone to write down their questions.

When all are finished, read aloud one question at a time and invite discussion. Share your own experiences with similar questions and admit what you do not know. Affirm the honest question with comments such as:

- "I've often wondered that too..."
- "There's an issue that's given me lots of problems..."
- "I once asked a friend the same question, and I've always remembered her response..."

Closing Prayer

Option 1

If you have made the Easter garden, place it where all can see and invite group members to imagine themselves there. As they see the risen Jesus, they meditate on these questions:

- What do you want to ask Jesus?
- What do you want to tell Jesus?

Allow several moments of silence, or play background music softly during the reflection. You may wish to conclude by singing the chorus of an Easter hymn popular in your parish. Or, you may teach and sing the Spanish refrain:

¡Resuscitó, resuscitó, resuscitó, alleluia! (Repeat.)

Option 2

Thomas called on Jesus with the names "My Lord and my God." Which names express our feelings and beliefs about Jesus?

- Stand in a circle and go around the circle with each person contributing a personal name for Jesus, such as "My friend," "My brother," "My guide." Conclude:
  — Jesus, you gave Thomas what he needed to believe. Give us what we need to believe. *Amen.*

Option 3

The leader begins a sentence-completion prayer, and invites each person to add to it:

- God, today I celebrate because...

Option 4

Stand in a circle. Invite each person to turn to the person on his or her right, bless that person with the sign of the cross on the forehead and say:

- Blessed are you who have not seen and yet have come to believe.

Sample Session on the Sacraments

One important purpose of this period is to break open the meaning of the sacraments that the children have recently received.

Baptism

Begin by singing a Baptismal hymn such as "Come to the Water," "You Have Been Baptized in Christ," or one used in your parish.

An appropriate reading might be Romans 6:3-11 from the Easter Vigil.

Then unpack the meaning of the liturgical experience the children have recently had. If it is helpful, watch a videocassette of their baptism and have them bring their pictures, baptismal garments, candles and other mementos to prompt memories and stir discussion. Ask the parents to explain why they wanted their children baptized, and what it meant to them to watch as their children were baptized. You may also want to view the videocassettes *Baptism-Sacrament of Belonging*. (*Bautismo* in Spanish) or *Called by Name* (*Llamado por Nombre*), from Ikonographics/St. Anthony Messenger Press, 1-800-488-0488.

Ask the children:
• What prominent symbol do you associate with baptism here? (water)

Lead the group in a brainstorming session about the destructive and positive aspects of water, recording their impressions on chalkboard or newsprint:

Destructive	*Life-giving*
floods	rain, drink
drowning	cleansing

The church believes that baptism has the same qualities: bringing life, cleansing; destroying sin. Invite guests (perhaps children baptized last year) to share how they have felt those effects in their lives since their baptism.

Eucharist

Begin with one of the eucharistic hymns usually sung in your parish.

Have children share their memories of receiving the eucharist for the first time, and the times they have received it since then. Again, if they have pictures or videocassette from the Easter Vigil, these may refresh their memories. Or, see the videocassette *Grandma's Bread*, (*El Pan de la Abuela*) from Ikonographics/St. Anthony Messenger Press, 1-800-488-0488. Among

the many scriptures from which you could choose are these:
• Deuteronomy 8:2-3, 14-16—God feeds the Israelites with manna in the desert.
• 1 Corinthians 10:16-17—We who eat the one loaf are one body.
• John 6:1-14; Luke 9:11-17—Jesus feeds five thousand people.
• John 6:51-58—Jesus calls himself the living bread.
• Mark 14:12-16, 22-26—Jesus gives himself to his friends through bread and wine at the Last Supper.

This sample session is based on John 21:1-19, the gospel for the Third Sunday of Easter, Year C.

After proclaiming the gospel ask:
• What did you hear?
• What did you like best in this story?
• How does it feel now that you can receive the eucharist too?

Invite the children to create modern versions of the gospel story such as this:

Imagine that you are struggling through a big test at school one day. Suddenly, a stranger appears at your side and says, "Here, use this pencil instead; you will know every answer." You begin writing with the stranger's pencil and discover he is right—you know every answer! You look up and realize the stranger is Jesus.
— How do you feel about Jesus?
— What do you want to say to him?

Encourage the children to talk about what the eucharist means to them. You may also want to invite guests (parents, godparents, sponsors, parish members) who have cher-

TIP: Party Time!

Organize a Pentecost picnic with the children that the neophytes will be with next year, either in parish religious education or the parish school. Or arrange a special eucharist for the neophytes, their families, and all who have celebrated first eucharist or confirmation during the Easter season.

ished the eucharist throughout their lives to tell the children why it is so important. You may invite some of the children or peer companions who received their first eucharist last year to describe their year of nourishment at the eucharistic table.

This would be a good time for children and their families to use *First Eucharist and Beyond* or *A Catechetical Guide to Gather Faithfully Together.* Sessions and participant papers for all age levels help children become "full, active and conscious participants" in the Mass because they understand its different parts, cultural adaptations, and links to daily life. Both resources available from Living the Good News, 1-800-824-1813.

If you have time for an art activity, make a banner titled, "We Share the Eucharist." Invite the children to use felt scraps and fabric markers to draw themselves at the eucharistic table. Fasten the top part of the banner over a dowel. You may want to hang it in your meeting place or have several children carry it in the entrance procession at Mass.

Confirmation

Pentecost is a good day to discuss confirmation. Begin by singing a hymn to the Holy Spirit.

Read the Pentecost account in Acts 2:1-11.

As you read, invite the children to close their eyes and imagine they are there in the upper room with the disciples. After the reading, ask:
- What did you see?
- What did you hear?

Then discuss:
- What was Jesus' gift to his friends?
- Why do you think Jesus gave them the Spirit?
- What difference did this event make in their lives?
- God gifts you with the Spirit too. How can that gift in confirmation change your attitudes? your actions?
- What are your special talents and abilities? How can you use these to serve God and others?

Here are three activities to follow up the Pentecost celebration if time permits:
- Invite a guest to talk about "The great things God has done in my life." How has the Spirit been active in this person's life?
- Pretend you work for the Jerusalem News. Invent an imaginary radio or television report on the events of Pentecost. Record it on audio or videocassette, play it back and enjoy.
- If the weather permits, move the session outside to enjoy the wind, with kites, pinwheels, balloons, wind streamers, bubbles, wind chimes, etc.

Notes

1. Thomas Morris, *THE RCIA: Transforming the Church* (New York: Paulist Press, 1997), 213.

Another resource on confirmation is *Confirmation: Anointed and Sealed with the Spirit* by Thomas Morris and Kathy Coffey. Leader Guide and participant journals are available from Living the Good News, 1-800-824-1813.

Chapter 10

Beyond Initiation

Jessica's Continuing Journey

Jessica enjoyed all the parties of mystagogy, especially the celebration of Pentecost, with its fuschia banners, hot pink streamers, fiery geraniums on the altar, fresh strawberries after Mass and pulsing music that sounded like wind:

   "Veni, Sancte Spiritus..."

She also felt special when she gathered with other newly baptized people to meet the bishop. She continued to meet with her group for a year, to talk about scripture, church tradition and the sacraments they had received. Making sandwiches for the

homeless was a regular part of Saturdays, and helping out at home became almost second nature. The first anniversary of her baptism was cause for another celebration with those who had shared that memorable night.

Several years afterward, Jessica became an energetic participant in the youth group, and later continued in adult religious education. Naturally, she hit snags along the way, and for a time during college, stayed away from church. Eventually, she returned to it, and her family life and profession became her ministry. Those first hesitant steps with Lupe by her side had led to

The newly baptized need to find in the parish community the experience and example of generous Christian love.

The most prized aspects of the catechumenate were feelings of community, friendship and acceptance.

an unending path. Mystagogy marks a beginning...

What can a parish do to enhance the neophyte's transition from an initiation group into the larger faith community? Parishes might evaluate themselves on how well they measure up to the *Rite's* directives about the newly initiated:

Could we say this of ourselves?
- "The whole community welcomes you with love and stands ready to help you" (*RCIA*, #55B).

How do we translate this into the practical aid offered by our unique parish?

Could we say this of our neophytes?
- "They... find in our community compelling signs of unity and generous love" (*RCIA*, #65).

During mystagogy, direct the neophytes to look for these signs, then discuss what they find—or don't find.

The *Rite* directs that the children gather with the Sunday assembly weekly and enter into reflection on their experience (*RCIA*, #330). A possible adaptation of ongoing mystagogy could be enrolling them in the parish's formal religious education program in addition to monthly gatherings with other neophytes.

Community Bonds

"Journey to the Fullness of Life" was the first comprehensive national study of the implementation of the *Rite* in the United States, authorized by the National Conference of Catholic Bishops. It provides data on the time after full initiation for adults

but not for children. So the data will need to be interpreted carefully in applying it to children. In that area, we have much to learn. Fifty-four percent of the adults surveyed continue to meet informally with their groups. The majority are happy with their parishes, and have a level of Mass attendance and involvement in parish ministries which is higher than the Catholic average.

"The most prized aspects of the catechumenate were feelings of community, friendship and acceptance. Responses indicate on balance that the human bonds and sentiments are cherished more than the instruction."[1] This information should comfort team members who worry that they haven't "covered enough material." If they have established caring relationships and begun a process that will unfold gradually, they have done the most important thing!

Some participants asked for more "aftercare" beyond initiation, and more study of doctrines, sacraments and moral teachings. While these were adult respondents, they can suggest a direction for children, in particular, after their full sacramental initiation. The time leading up to the celebration of the initiation sacraments with children, with its community building activities, scripture study, prayer and preparation for the rites, is simply overflowing with doctrinal teachings. And, of course, there is abundant time after initiation for more intensive and life-long formation.

Adults who have enjoyed the closeness and camaraderie of a small initiation group may feel overwhelmed by a large parish in which they know few people. Often, they join small Christian communities which meet their need for ongoing faith sharing and community. While some of these are intergenerational, it may take some creative planning on the part of the initiation team to find or establish similar groups for children. While the director may not want one more burden in an already full schedule, the formation and maintenance of a "small Christian community" for newly initiated children might be undertaken by their parents or sponsors. At a minimum, children may want to exchange addresses, phone numbers, or e-mail addresses. They should also celebrate the anniversary of their initiation every year.

The Uses of Enchantment

Remember that an important dimension of "aftercare" is the beauty, poetry and mystery which first attracted the children to the church. As you continue to strengthen their relationships and integrate them into the community, provide opportunities to nurture the soul. As Cardinal Godfried Danneels writes, "I ask myself whether we are using sufficiently one of the doors that leads to God—the door named Beauty." He points out that for contemporary people, beauty is disarming and irresistible. The church has a long heritage of art, music, literature and "saints who shone with beauty."[2]

What this means for children may vary according to their particular sensitivities. Give them a broad overview of their Catholic artistic heritage, then guide them deeper into the areas where they are drawn. A field trip to the library might be a fine mystagogical experience. Enlist there the help of librarians or parents who may specialize in storytelling, music, the arts or sciences.

For children with an interest in the performing arts, see if your parish, a neighboring one or the local school offers opportunities for choir, dance or drama. Children's singing or dancing can enliven liturgy, and attract friends or relatives who might not otherwise attend church! Guiding children to identify and develop their natural gifts not only enhances them; it enriches the whole community.

Catholic Means Universal

Throughout the catechumenate process, you have tried to introduce children to multi-cultural dimensions of the religious experience. After their full initiation, you may have more time to continue this exposure. If the children in your group come primarily from one ethnic background, arrange for them to visit a church of a different ethnic mix: African-American, Hispanic, Anglo or Asian. Advance planning will enable them not only to attend a liturgy, but also to meet other children in the initiation process, and share a potluck meal or do an activity together. Again, enlist parents and sponsors from both parishes to help with this effort.

Another good project is to discover the stories of saints or heroes in different cultures. Many stories that were once obscure are now available to us. Find books and art appropriate for children; invite them to do some research, then to dramatize or draw "los santos." Remember to keep this project vibrant, interactive, multi-sensory, not a boring study of the dead.

Ask children to also be sensitive to the saints who live around them—a teacher, a grandpa, a neighbor, a friend, a cousin, a shop owner, a coach.

You may also wish to use Sister Wendy's popular books on art for children.

Empowering the Parents

Many initiation team members and directors grow fond of children during the catechumenate, and are saddened when their time of formal initiation draws to a close. But they find that the best way to continue the process is to educate and empower the children's parents.

The church teaches that parents have the primary responsibility for religious education. Even the finest parish ministry must be reinforced at home, or the child will spend too much time living in a vacuum. If parents have been directly involved with their children's initiation, have been initiated themselves, or have participated in intergenerational catechesis, they are better equipped for this responsibility.

The initiation team has modeled for them how to appreciate children's spirituality, adapt to different learning styles and cultures, pray spontaneously and lead rituals. Parents who have participated in sessions that break open God's word should be able to have similar conversations about faith with their children. Because they have taken part in service projects, they know the importance of continuing these with their families.

Parents will still face tough questions and doubts but the preparation and support given by the parish should enhance their confidence. Furthermore, they have formed relationships with parish staff and parishioners to whom they can turn if a problem is more than they can handle alone. Some people simply need encouragement a reminder of how important parenting is and assurance of the community resources that can help them. If your parish has ongoing adult/intergenerational education or retreats, encourage the neophytes' parents to participate, providing schedules and information about child care and transportation.

Continuing Apprenticeship

As we said in Chapter Two, the goal of full initiation is an apprenticeship to Christ that becomes a life-long process. Conversion is an ongoing process; we mentor children into a way of life. The practices begun during the catechumenate should be continued: reading the scripture, a continued exposure to various forms of communal and personal prayer, outreach. We also continue to feed the senses with beauty: brass, string and choral music, colorful textures, incense, candles and flowers. If possible, invite the children to be part of liturgical preparation: baking bread, preparing the general intercessions, decorating the church, bringing up the gifts.

Finally, we remember that Christ who began the good work in these children will bring it to completion (Philippians 1:6). Thankful that we have played some part in their conversion, we place them in the compassionate hands of our God. Then directors, team members, parents and sponsors can share the fulfillment promised by Daniel 12:3: "Those who instruct others to justice shall shine as stars for all eternity."

Notes

1. "Journey to the Fullness of Life," 6.

2. Godfried Danneels, "The Contemporary Person and the Church," *America* (July 30-August 6, 2001), 9.

Resources for Further Reading

On the Spirituality of Children

Cavalletti, Sofia. *The Religious Potential of the Child.* Chicago: Liturgy Training Publications, 1992.

Coles, Robert. *The Spiritual Life of Children.* Boston: Houghton Mifflin, 1990.

Coffey, Kathy. *Experiencing God with your Children.* New York: Crossroad, 1997.

Fitzpatrick, Jean. *Something More: Nurturing Your Child's Spiritual Growth.* New York: Viking, 1991.

Fowler, James. *The Stages of Faith.* San Francisco: Harper and Row, 1981.

Kiersey, David and Marilyn Bates. *Please Understand Me.* Gnosology Books, 1984.

Pipher, Mary. *The Shelter of Each Other.* New York: Ballantine Books, 1996.

Westerhoff, John. *Will Our Children Have Faith?* Harrisburg: Morehouse Press, 2000.

On the Rite of Christian Initiation of Children

Bernstein, Eleanor and John Brooks-Leonard, eds. *Children in the Assembly of the Church.* Chicago: Liturgy Training Publications, 1992.

Brown, Kathy and Frank Sokol. *Issues in the Christian Initiation of Children.* Chicago: Liturgy Training Publications, 1989.

International Commission on English in the Liturgy. *Rite of Christian Initiation of Adults.* Study Edition. Collegeville, MN: Order of St. Benedict, 1988.

Kelly, Maureen and Robert Duggan. *The Christian Initiation of Children: Hope for the Future.* Mahwah, NJ: Paulist Press, 1991.

Mitchell, Nathan. *Eucharist as Sacrament of Initiation.* Chicago: Liturgy Training Publications, 1994.

Morris, Thomas. *The RCIA: Transforming the Church.* New York: Paulist Press, 1997.

Searle, Mark. *The Church Speaks About Sacraments with Children.* Chicago: Liturgy Training Publications, 1990.

Senseman, Rita Burns. *A Child's Journey: the Christian Initiation of Children.* Cincinnati: St. Anthony Messenger Press, 1998.

Victoria Tufano, ed. *Readings in the Christian Initiation of Children.* Chicago: Liturgy Training Publications, 1994.

On Family Prayer

A Prayer Book for Catholic Families. Chicago: Loyola Press, 1998.

Curran, Dolores. *On Family Prayer.* Mystic, CT: Twenty-Third Publications, 1997.

Denham, Joyce, ed. *A Child's Book of Celtic Prayers.* Chicago: Loyola Press, 1998.

Finley, Kathleen. *Our Family Book of Days.* St. Mary's Press, 1997.

Knickerbocker, Lynne and others. *Parent Child Retreats: Spiritual Experiences for Children Ages 7-10 and Their Parents.* Denver: Living the Good News, 1998.

Linn, Dennis, Sheila and Matthew. *Sleeping with Bread.* New York: Paulist Press, 1995.

―――. *Healing the Purpose of Your Life.* New York: Paulist Press, 1999.

Videocassettes

Neumann, Don. *The Catechumenate for Children.* Allen, TX: Tabor Publishing.

―――. *This Is the Night.* Chicago: Liturgy Training Publications.

Sunday Morning. Chicago: Liturgy Training Publications.

Glossary

Candidate: a baptized person who is preparing for confirmation and eucharist to be received into the full communion of the Catholic church. At the time of full reception, he or she will make a profession of faith, be confirmed, and receive eucharist.

Catechesis: suitable pastoral formation and guidance, aimed at training catechumens in the Christian life (*RCIA*, #75.) "The goal of catechesis is to put people in touch, in communion, indeed, in intimacy, with Jesus Christ" (*GDC*, #80. See also *CCC*, #426). "Authentic catechesis is always an orderly and systematic initiation into the revelation that God has given of himself to humanity in Christ Jesus" (*GDC*, #66).

Catechumen: an unbaptized person who is preparing for all three sacraments of initiation.

Catechumenate: "This is the time, in duration corresponding to the progress of the individual, for the nurturing and growth of the catechumens' faith and conversion to God; celebrations of the word and prayers of exorcism and blessing are meant to assist the process" (*RCIA*, Part I [after #35]). "The place where catechesis occurs in the handing on of the gospels" (*GDC*, #88).

Conscience: Conscience is a way of judging or discerning whether or not the general contours of a person's life are in harmony with God's will and whether or not certain actions, omissions or attitudes clash with moral principle (*CCC*, 1776–94).

Conversion: "the full and sincere adherence to the person of Christ and the decision to walk in his footsteps" (*GDC*, #17).

Ecumenism: "This term refers to the spirit and principles that guide Christian communities and individuals in their efforts to heal the scandal of schism and division in the Church" (*GDC*, #86 and *CCC*, #197–98).

The Elect: those chosen by God to celebrate the sacraments of initiation.

Evangelization: faithfully proclaiming the living God and Jesus whom God sent for our salvation (*RCIA*, #36). It varies, based on its audience, occurs in "sacred moments" and unfolds slowly (*GDC*, #49). In this process, human words point to divine works.

Initiation: the process by which a person converts to a relationship with Jesus Christ.

Inquirers: people who are inquiring about the Catholic faith and participate in the pre-catechumenate.

Liturgical catechesis: The activity of bringing communal faith to consciousness through participation in and celebration of the rites of the community. Through the mediation of symbols and the celebration of rites, one is immersed in and touched by a mystery deeper and more radical than the event itself.

Liturgy: the official public worship of the Church, especially eucharist and the sacraments.

Lectionary: The liturgical book of readings that contains the scriptures for Sundays and feast days of the church calendar.

Lectionary Catechesis: An understanding of a particular scripture text within the context of the liturgical celebration and the liturgical year.

Minor Rites: the exorcisms, blessings and anointings which occur during the period of catechumenate.

Mystagogy: teaching the mysteries, (*mysta* meaning 'mystery' and *gogia* meaning 'teaching'). The fourth and final period in the order of Christian initiation, after full sacramental initiation, which emphasizes "the experience of the sacraments themselves and entry into community life" (*GDC*, #88).

Neophytes: the newly initiated.

Precatechumenate: "This is a time, of no fixed duration or structure, for inquiry and introduction to Gospel values, an opportunity for the beginnings of faith" (*RCIA*, Part I [after #35]). "This is the early and initial turning of one's life to Christ and the truths of the gospel" (*GDC*, #88).

Presentations: giving the Creed and the Lord's Prayer to candidates and catechumens through special rites during purification and enlightenment or, if appropriate, during the catechumenate period.

Purification and Enlightenment: "The time immediately preceding the elects' initiation, usually the Lenten season preceding the celebration of this initiation at the Easter Vigil; it is a time of reflection, intensely centered on conversion, marked by celebration of the scrutinies and presentations and of the preparation rites on Holy Saturday" (*RCIA*, Part I [after #35]). "the more intense period of preparation for the sacraments of initiation where the Creed and the Lord's Prayer take center stage" (*GDC*, #88).

Scrutiny: Scrutiny means a close examination, a careful looking-over. It does not "point the finger" at one person, but is a community task of looking at how evil affects our lives and finding how we can be liberated from it by Christ's grace.

Triduum: the solemn celebration that begins with the Mass of the Lord's Supper on Holy Thursday and concludes on Easter Sunday. During this time we celebrate Jesus' passion, death and resurrection.

A Calendar of Celebrations

The church year is rich in seasons and cycles, balancing feasts and fasts, highs and lows. There is almost always something to celebrate. As the mystic Hildegard of Bingen wrote in the fourteenth century, "Be not lax in celebrating. Be not lazy in the festive service of God. Be ablaze with enthusiasm."

Parents with tight schedules might worry how they can squeeze in one more thing, but these celebrations need not be long or complicated. Gradually giving the child responsibility for the preparation instills a sense of ownership and relieves some of the burden on mom or dad's time. Nielsen surveys found that the average American household watches television for over 25 hours a week. Surely a few moments for a religious observance can be a more rewarding use of time.

What follows offers some suggestions for household celebration. But note that adult modeling is crucial. If the children see parents joyously absorbed in the celebration, they know it is important for them to participate too. Their radar is set for interesting stuff: if adults show enthusiasm and enjoyment, it becomes contagious.

The church year doesn't follow a calendar year or an academic year. Instead it begins with Advent and culminates with the Feast of Christ the King. The Sunday readings for a whole year give the full story of Christ's life and the unfolding of the mystery of our salvation.

Advent

The First Sunday of Advent usually occurs during the last week of November or the first week of December. The Advent season extends through four weeks, culminating in Christmas.

December 3—St. Francis Xavier

This Jesuit missionary preached to the Hindus, Malayans and Japanese. On a map or globe, find where their modern descendants might live. Francis respected their unique cultures; borrow a library book on how they live today.

December 6—St. Nicholas

Children who put their shoes outside their doors the night before find candy and small toys there in the morning. They can also be "little Nicholases," secretly doing kindnesses for each other.

December 8—Feast of the Immaculate Conception

Mary was filled with grace from her conception, and thus suited for the unique role in human salvation that would be hers. In honor of Jesus' mother, pray together her hymn of praise, the Magnificat (Luke 1:46-55).

December 12—Our Lady of Guadalupe

Read the children's version of the story by Tomie dePaola: *The Lady of Guadalupe.*

December 13—St. Lucy (whose name means light)

Adapt the Swedish custom of the oldest daughter wearing a crown of candles and carrying a tray of breakfast rolls to her family the morning of the feast.

December 16—Las Posadas

For the nine days before Christmas, Spanish-speaking people re-enact Mary and Joseph's quest for a place their child could be born. The procession is denied entrance at every home, until at last, one welcomes them and a party with piñatas begins.

Christmas

December 24—Christmas Eve

Traditions celebrated on Christmas Eve provide some of the year's most unforgettable moments. Some families have a special reading of the nativity story, others have a special meal; others place a figure of the Christ Child in the crib or the crèche.

December 26-January 1—Kwanzaa

On each of the seven days, African-Americans light a candle reaffirming seven principles: unity, self-determination, responsibility, cooperative economics, purpose, creativity and faith.

December 26—St. Stephen

Stephen became the first martyr of the church when he boldly spoke for Jesus and angered the temple authorities. Tell stories of those who speak out boldly in our own day.

December 28—Feast of the Holy Innocents

These little boys were slain by Herod in his murderous attempt to kill the Christ Child. Some European countries call this "Children's Day" and put children in charge of planning activities and games.

December 31—New Year's Eve

A good time to take stock of the past year and especially to thank God for all the blessings it brought.

January 1—Mary the Mother of God

Today we begin the new civil year remembering Mary as the mother of our newborn Savior and as the woman "full of grace." She models how each of us can give birth to the Christ Child in our time and place.

January 4—St. Elizabeth Ann Seton

The widowed mother of five small children, she was the first saint born in the United States to be canonized by the Catholic Church. Two of her daughters died in childhood, but despite her grief, Seton went on to found the first North American parish school, religious community and orphanage. She could be the patron saint of single parents.

A Moveable Celebration—Hanukkah, the Eight Day Festival of Lights

In the Jewish tradition, families light the menorah, one candle each night for eight nights, and play games with dreidels or spinning tops.

Lent

All of Lent is a preparation for Easter, when we celebrate the events of Jesus' passion, death and resurrection. The timing of Lent (the 40 days before Easter) will vary each year, but will often include the following dates:

March 7 — Sts. Perpetua and Felicity

Perpetua and her servant Felicity were two African martyrs who are mentioned in the Eucharistic Prayer at Mass. Perpetua, age 22, recorded little dismay at Roman brutality, but much concern for her infant son. When she got permission to have the baby in jail with her, she wrote that her prison had become a palace.

March 17 — St. Patrick

He went to Ireland in 431 as a missionary and spent the rest of his life there as bishop, educator and defender of Christianity. Wear green.

March 19 — St. Joseph

Read the children's book, *Song of the Swallows* by Leo Politi, about the custom of the swallows returning to Capistrano every year on this feast.

March 24 — Archbishop Oscar Romero

He was killed in El Salvador while saying Mass on this day in 1980. During his final homily, this modern martyr spoke about injustice: "We must do what we can. All of us can do something." If an older child has not seen the film *Romero*, rent it and view it together.

March 25 — Annunciation

When God wanted to become human, God didn't consult a panel of theological experts or government officials. God asked a girl of about 14. She said yes. To celebrate Jesus' conception, a mini-Christmas in Lent, bake Christmas cookies or sing a Christmas carol.

April 22 — Earth Day

Stewardship of the earth is essential to the Catholic tradition. If your child doesn't have a copy of *Fifty Things Kids Can Do to Save the Earth*, get one and choose a project from it to do today.

April 25 — St. Mark

In Mark's gospel (8:29), Jesus looks us straight in the eye and asks, "Who do you say that I am?" And we answer?

Holy Week

This week presents a superb opportunity to quiet all the external noise and spend special time with Jesus. For instance, look at a calendar. Choose a week and try to recount the events that happened during those seven days. Then talk about what happened to Jesus during the final week of his life. What might he have been thinking or feeling each day as he drew closer to his death? What might his friends have been going through? Explain that you will imagine yourself there with Jesus during Holy Week. As we share his last journey, it is a powerful reminder that he is always with us.

Palm Sunday

One day the people of Jerusalem welcomed Jesus with shouts of praise and cloaks thrown on the ground; the next, they planned to crucify him. Re-enacting their drama, think of how easily people can join in popular slogans and forget individual responsibility. It might be a good time to talk with children about peer pressure: When does it influence them to do things they'd rather not? How can they resist it?

Many churches celebrate this feast with a procession in which people carry palms or greenery. Some parishes invite the children to lead the procession.

The Easter Triduum (Three Days)

Holy Thursday

After you attend the Holy Thursday liturgy, talk about each part and what it meant to the children:

- the washing of feet—Explain that the custom was required originally by the dusty roads on which Jesus and his disciples walked. However, washing feet was usually the task of women or slaves. When Jesus did it himself, he gave us a powerful example of service: not lording it over others, but performing the lowliest jobs for them. Talk about Jesus' gesture in the context of the ministry the child has done this year.
- the stories of the Israelites escaping destruction (Exodus 12:1-8, 11 14) and of Jesus' final evening with his friends (John 13:1-15).
- the procession to the altar of repose—The ancient roots of this procession of the blessed sacrament remind us that the ground on which we walk is holy.
- stripping the altar—The cross and candlesticks, the altar cloths and flowers are all removed. The sanctuary light is extinguished. The church seems hollow and empty. How does this make you feel?

Passover Memories

If your parish has a Seder meal, try to participate. It will help the child understand the Jewish roots of Jesus' last meal. If this is not possible, you can at least sample some Passover foods. Explain that Passover celebrates the liberation of the Jewish people from slavery. They remember how God sent Moses to lead the Hebrews out of Egypt. Jesus shared the Passover meal with his disciples the night before he died. The following foods are similar to those he might have had, and ingredients should not be hard to find in your local grocery store. As you prepare and eat them, tell the stories of their origins:

- matzo bread—a flat, unleavened bread. The Hebrews made it without yeast because they had to leave Egypt quickly. They had no time to let the bread rise (Exodus 12:39).
- haroses—chopped apples and nuts mixed with honey, which may be eaten between pieces of matzo bread. Its color reminds us of the bricks made by the Hebrew people when they were slaves in Egypt.
- horseradish—a bitter taste, a reminder of how bitter slavery is. (Add a tiny dab to the matzo and haroses.)
- grape juice or wine—reminder of the lamb's blood that was sprinkled on the doorposts of Israelite homes as a sign to spare them from plague (Exodus 12:13).

Good Friday

This is the most solemn day of the church year, when we remember the brutal crucifixion of Jesus. We remember how much he loved us, even unto death. The symbol of the cross takes some of our worst fears—of betrayal, torture, pain and death—and turns them into an expression of hope. Christians voice confidence that Jesus has conquered sin and death. We find meaning in our sufferings because they are linked to Christ's.

Here are ways to commemorate this day:

Reading the Passion
On Passion/Palm Sunday, the story of Jesus' passion is told.

The whole passion story may be too much for some children to absorb. If this is the case for your child, choose a few episodes and focus on these. Do an activity to help the child enter into one of the shorter segments of the story.

Questions for Discussing the Passion Story
- How did Jesus' friends turn their backs on him? How have I?
- What part of Jesus' suffering do you think was the hardest?
- Why did Jesus endure such suffering and death?
- Knowing how Jesus suffered and died, what would you like to say to him now? (Pause for quiet prayer if it seems appropriate.)
- Explain the custom of reverencing or kissing the cross. Through this gesture, we not only embrace Christ's suffering, but our own particular cross. For love of him, we take up this burden anew.

Possibilities for Art
- Provide materials such as cardboard boxes, scraps of paper and cloth, foil, pipe cleaners, construction paper, scissors, glue and crayons or felt markers. With the child, make a table-top scene to illustrate one event of Holy Week. You might title the scene and discuss contemporary applications:
  — Where is Jesus tried in court today?
  — Where does Jesus fall today?
  — Who reaches out to comfort him today?

Holy Saturday
Prepare for full sacramental initiation at the Easter Vigil.

Baptismal Candle
Make or decorate the baptismal candle that the child and the godparent will hold. It is a symbol of the child's faith in Christ, burning bright. You may want to gather with other parents, godparents and sponsors for this preparation. Beforehand, assemble these materials:
   paraffin wax or old candles, clean, empty cans, hot plate, electric frying pan or hot water, brushes, plain candle to decorate, small leaves and flowers.

To shape the candles, melt paraffin or old candles in empty cans, using the hot plate, frying pan or hot water. While still hot, insert string for wick. When cooled, decorate the candle:
- by arranging small leaves and delicate flowers in a pleasing design. Use a brush dipped in liquid wax to seal each leaf or flower to the candle.
- or by carving into it with a heated knife the child's name and the date, or symbols that are special to the child, for example, water or a vine.
- or by attaching small flowers or grasses to a ready-made candle, then brushing over them with melted wax to make them adhere.

Baptismal Name

Review the significance of the baptismal name. The child may already be familiar with the importance of names through the rite of election. The word name is found some 850 times in the Hebrew scriptures. The worst curse that the Jews could utter was "may your name be blotted out." The greatest blessing was for a person's name to be remembered through descendants. A name represents a person's presence and power. If your child is choosing a baptismal name or using the name given at birth, help him or her discover what it means. Assure the child that God calls each of us by name.

As full initiation comes closer, you walk a fine line: wanting to prepare the child for the "spine-tingling rites," yet at the same time, not overpreparing, so that the child comes to the ritual experience fresh and tastes it fully. Even though the rites may not go perfectly and the children may not seem to fully comprehend them, grace can still carry the day!

Easter Season

Celebrations at home should relate to the Sunday eucharist, because now the child can come to the table. During the fifty days of the Easter season, choose an activity to do or a feast to celebrate. More important than creating a perfect artwork is the time spent together and the opportunity it offers for discussion. As you work, discuss memories of the Easter Vigil, your own experiences of resurrection, or what Easter means to the Christian community. One of the easiest things you can do is use a traditional Easter greeting.

Easter Tree

Find a bare or flowering branch outdoors and anchor it in a flowerpot with sand or pebbles. Place it in a prominent place in your home, then decorate it with a variety of Easter symbols. Some possible decorations:

- Eggshell ornaments: Make a tiny hole in each end of a raw egg. Blow through the hole to force the egg white and yolk into a bowl. Then draw on the shell with felt pens or colored pencils. Hang the eggshell on the branch with ribbon.
- Small figures such as angels, made from pipe cleaners and attached to the tree with ribbon.
- Tiny baskets filled with green Easter grass.
- Miniature wooden figures of birds, butterflies, etc., sold at craft shops.

Easter Scavenger Hunt

This project would be fun with several children, so ask friends and siblings to join in. Some items you might ask the children to find.

- The liturgical color for Easter is white. Find something white.
- We celebrate Easter in spring. Find a sign of spring.
- During this season, the paschal candle burns throughout our liturgies. Find a candle.
- During this season, we celebrate the Feast of the Good Shepherd. Find a picture of a sheep or shepherd.
- Jesus rose to bring us new life. Find a symbol of new life.

Feasts of the Season

While the official period of mystagogy extends through the fifty days between Easter and Pentecost, feasts beyond that time span are included here for those who want to continue celebrating some wonderful feasts in summer.

April 29 — St. Catherine of Siena

Despite the turbulence of constant warfare in 14th-century Italy, she developed a rich inner life as a child. Her sturdy sense of self seemed to spring from her parents' cherishing her (one of 25 children!). Though she relished prayerful solitude, Jesus told her, "Your neighbors are the channel through which all your virtues come to birth."

May 1 — St. Joseph the Worker

Human beings are like God when they create: from wood or words, paints or plants, songs or sopapillas. Today we celebrate the dignity of work, the sanctity possible even in the most ordinary circumstances.

May 15 — Sts. Isidore and Maria

They are one of the few married couples canonized by the church. Farmers in 12th-century Spain, they are now the patrons of the Catholic Rural Life Conference. They remind urban as well as rural people that we stand on holy ground. Plant some vegetable seeds, flowers or saplings in their honor today.

Moveable Feasts

Ascension (40 days after Easter Sunday)

While this feast marks the end of Jesus' physical presence with the disciples, we do not gaze at the heavens and mourn his departure. Instead we celebrate our own sending forth as witnesses who do his work on earth.

Pentecost (50 days after Easter Sunday)

This feast was discussed in the context of confirmation, but here are a few more ways to celebrate it.

- Wear fiery colors (crimson, fuchsia, hot pink).
- Learn the Our Father in another language.
- Compliment family members on their unique gifts of the Spirit.
- Decorate with red geraniums; feast on fresh strawberries.
- Pray over children: "Do not fear to set fire to the world; discover and live the wonderful works of God."
- Learn the prayer: "Come, Holy Spirit, fill the hearts of your faithful and kindle in them the fire of your love."

Trinity Sunday (one week after Pentecost)

If the concept of a trinitarian God is difficult for most adults, it must be doubly so for children. To make the belief more concrete, shape from clay Trinity symbols such as a triangle, a shamrock or three interlocking circles.

Body and Blood of Christ (one week after Trinity Sunday)

Try a new variety of bread today. Write a poem about bread or paint a mural of you, your friends and family at a banquet with Jesus. Complete these acrostics by filling in words that start with each of these letters.

B	W
R	I
E	N
A	E
D	

Sacred Heart (Friday following Body and Blood of Christ)

St. Margaret Mary Alacoque urged this feast to make reparation for human ingratitude. The symbol of the heart represents Jesus' unconditional love, which is neither deserved nor earned, but which every child (and adult) longs for.

Feasts of Ordinary Time

May 26 — St. Philip Neri

His two favorite books were the New Testament and a collection of riddles and jokes. All his biographers mention his lively sense of humor. When he was ordained, he said Mass with a chipmunk on his shoulder, and refused to become a bishop. He left us two pieces of good advice:
- "Don't be forever dwelling on your sins. Leave a little something for the angels."
- "I will have no sadness in my house."

Celebrate his spirit by telling jokes today.

May 27 — St. Augustine of Canterbury

He was sent to convert England in 596, but made a U-turn back to Rome because he was terrified of the ferocity of the Anglo-Saxons. Sent back to England by Pope Gregory the Great, he learned to incorporate local customs into Christian feasts. His failures and compromises encourage us to continue despite frustrations and set-backs.

May 31 — The Visitation

Read, roleplay or act out with puppets this story (Luke 1:39-45) of Mary visiting her relative, Elizabeth. Learn to sing or say a few verses of Mary's Magnificat, outlawed by some South American dicta-torships because it is a subversive song of liberation.

June 3 — St. Charles Lwanga and the Ugandan Martyrs

They were martyred as young converts and canonized in 1964. How much do you and your child know about current conditions in Africa? This might be a good day to read a news report or watch a documentary together.

June 11 — St. Barnabas

Barnabas, whose name means "son of encouragement," is a special patron of initiation sponsors. He persuaded the Christian community to accept Paul, who had once persecuted Christians murderously. They probably never dreamed what gifts the transformed Paul would bring them! He also accompanied Paul on his missionary journeys.

June 22 — St. Thomas More, the Man for All Seasons

Rent the video by that title and admire the courage of this chancellor of England who stood up to his king on principle. He was beheaded for treason and died "the king's good servant, but God's first." The father of four, More joked that the executioner should spare his beard, because at least it had done no wrong.

June 24 — St. John the Baptist

A good time for review: do you remember this odd herald who ate locusts and honey and first appeared in the Advent gospels —over six months ago?

June 29 — Sts. Peter and Paul

Both these glorious apostles had a history of mistakes and denials. Their propensity to failure should encourage even the shakiest new Christian.

July 1—St. Junipero Serra

A string of missions along the California coast pays tribute to the zeal of this Franciscan. His "Regulation" protecting Native Americans was the basis for the first significant state legislation, their bill of rights.

July 3—St. Thomas

Today is the feast of the holy doubter whose story is told on the Second Sunday of Easter.

July 14—St. Kateri Tekakwitha

She was the first Native American to be canonized. An Iroquois girl, she often meditated on the great dignity of being baptized and drew strength from her Christian community.

July 22—St. Mary Magdalene

She stood by the cross and was the first witness to the resurrection. Tell the story of her mistaking Christ for the gardener outside his tomb.

July 29—St. Martha

She criticized her sister, Mary, for not helping with meal preparations, and rudely reminded Jesus that if he had answered her call sooner, her brother would not have died. Furthermore, she reminded him that a corpse would stink after four days. Her boldest stroke was affirming the resurrection and Jesus' identity as the Messiah (John 11:24-27).

July 31—St. Ignatius of Loyola

He founded the Jesuits, wrote the *Spiritual Exercises* still used in many retreat centers and the prayer: "Take Lord, receive, my memory, my understanding, my whole life...Give me only your love and your grace, that's enough for me."

August 11—St. Clare of Assisi

She was the lifelong friend of St. Francis and foundress of the Poor Clares, a contemplative religious order. Children might enjoy the video about them, *Brother Sun, Sister Moon.*

August 15—The Assumption of Mary

The doctrine of Mary's bodily assumption into heaven gives us the opportunity to celebrate the feminine, motherhood and the holiness of nature. Appropriately, it coincides with the season of harvest. Many communities bless their fruits and flowers on this day; do so using Psalm 65.

August 27—St. Monica

She is a model for parents because of her struggle to bring her son Augustine to the Christian faith. (His feast is August 28.) While we may want instant answers, she prayed and persevered for years until she saw the conversion of her licentious husband, cantankerous mother-in-law and famous, brilliant son.

September 9—St Peter Claver

He was a Spanish Jesuit who ministered to African slaves in Cartagena (now Colombia) as they arrived for work in the mines. Conditions on the ships were deplorable, yet he brought medicine, food and drink there. More importantly, he tried to restore a sense of the person's dignity. What do you think he meant by saying, "deeds come first, then the words"?

September 21 — St. Matthew the Evangelist

Tradition identifies him as a reformed tax collector. He wrote the Good News of Jesus' life, death and resurrection, and is patron of the church's mission. Read a verse from his gospel today.

September 27 — St. Vincent de Paul

He became a priest to escape the poverty of his farm, and later became chaplain to one of Paris's wealthiest families. But in mid-life he decided to devote himself to the poor, and founded an order, the Vincentians, for the training of parish clergy. With the help of Louise de Marillac, he founded the Daughters of Charity, an order of women who weren't cloistered, but served the poor in the sickrooms and streets of the city.

October 1 — St. Thérèse of Lisieux

Also known as the "little flower," she lived a short, uneventful life, but is known for her "everyday" path to holiness, called the "Little Way." Read a child's biography of Thérèse this week.

October 4 — St. Francis of Assisi

He delighted in all God's creation. If your parish holds a blessing of the animals, attend. Or read Francis's "Canticle to the Sun."

October 15 — St. Teresa of Ávila

She was a mystic, spiritual writer, and great reformer. In 1970, she was the first woman named a Doctor of the Church.

November 1 — All Saints Day

Today we celebrate all baptized persons, living and dead, who make up the Body of Christ. This "cloud of witnesses" shares the divine energy, participates in the holiness of God and companions us along the way.

November 2 — All Souls Day

Today is set aside to remember and pray for the dead. Spanish-speaking areas have special customs for this day; participate in one of these.

November 3 — St. Martin de Porres

He was the illegitimate son of a Spanish nobleman and a black freed slave, who became a Dominican brother. He carried his healing ministry to the streets of Lima, Peru. Today send a card to or phone someone who's sick.

November 16 — The Martyrs of El Salvador

On this day in 1989, six Jesuits, their cook and her daughter were brutally murdered in El Salvador. From the University of Central America, they had consistently denounced the military regime who terrorized the people and perpetuated poverty. They paid the price for their bold stand.